THOUGHTS
OF TWO
WORLDS

THOUGHTS OF TWO WORLDS

JANUS PUBLISHING COMPANY
London, England

First published in Great Britain 1993
by Janus Publishing Company
Duke House
37 Duke Street
London W1M 5DF

Copyright © George Knight 1993

**British Library Cataloguing-in-Publication Data.
A catalogue record for this book is available
from the British Library.**

ISBN 1 85756 004 3

Cover design Optigraph
Printed & bound in England by Antony Rowe Ltd,
Chippenham, Wiltshire.

Contents

Preface

The words in this book on spiritual matters first started out as thoughts, inspiration brought to us by those who have passed from this world we call earth. Because they come from more than one person the word 'we' is used rather than 'I'.

There is a story of a small girl who when asked by her mother how she conversed with her 'dead' brother replied, 'We speak with our thinks.' The words written here are inspired by other people's 'thinks'.

We do not expect everyone who reads these thoughts to agree with them but we hope and indeed feel that there is something in them from which the reader can gain comfort, knowledge and inspiration. A spark that will make them think.

Many thanks go to all those who have helped and inspired me, especially my wife for all her efforts, so that this book could be published.

George Knight

1
Inspiration

Relaxation

Man today has more labour-saving devices than he has ever had in history and because of these inventions he should have more leisure time than ever before, but has he? We find him chasing about without a minute to breathe and no time to stand and stare.

At times we ridicule the people of Eastern countries because of their attitude to life and their patient or at times lazy way of living. We have never forgotten the story of the Chinese gentleman who wanted to catch a particular train and so called a taxi to take him to the station. The driver dashed away as fast as he could and when they arrived at the station said, 'There you are, sir, you have twenty minutes to spare,' and the reply was 'And what do you propose I do with them?' That is typical of life today.

We dash from one place to another and when we arrive we are at a loss as what to do because we have to wait for events to catch up with us or, if you like, we have to wait for the train to arrive. This is the difference between our way of life and the apparent lazy way of the Eastern nations. While we are waiting for the train we become impatient upsetting our nerves and possibly other people's as well.

We must cultivate patience – the quality of endurance in suffering injuries or injustice without anger or discount. When we have developed patience we are halfway to success and the next aim is relaxation because we cannot possibly relax if we are impatient.

Once we went to a school prize-giving ceremony where the speaker was a world-famous cricketer who said during his speech that the most important thing in his career was relaxation. He said to have ability was marvellous but to use it to the best of one's efforts required relaxation. We would say that relaxation is the most important thing in any and in everything we do – especially spiritual matters.

When we sit in developing circles to learn about spiritual matters and do not seem to be making much progress, we blame all sorts of things. Could it be our own fault because we are not patient or relaxed enough? Let us remember that in a circle each sitter has a certain quality to offer that must blend in with the other sitters' qualities. Sometimes we have to move to other circles because our guides feel we should move to a higher development. Whatever circle we sit in we must relax, but how do we do this? How can we shut out the material or, to put in another way, how do we develop mind over matter?

We were once told to imagine a stone being thrown into a pool of water and watch the ripples it made from the centre to the edges or we could look at a rose and concentrate our thoughts on how the petals were made.

As we started to speak in public we used to suffer agonies and in a lot of instances were physically sick before leaving home. Some would say it was nerves, perhaps we wanted to go too fast too soon, perhaps we were concerned about not giving a good enough service but whatever the reason, we certainly were not relaxed enough. The amazing thing was that as soon as the service began we were all right.

In the material aspect of life we do not always get the things we want and those that we do receive we have to work and wait for. It is the same spiritually because we cannot be fortunate like Saul of Tarsus and have our desires given to us in a flash of light.

Sometimes we are given messages which tell us to watch a certain time but when that time arrives nothing appears to have happened and so we say the message was wrong. Could it be that an opportunity presented itself but we missed it? There was a gentleman who received such a message and to outsiders nothing happened but that gentleman, acting on thoughts that came into his head, made a decision that altered his whole life. Therefore before we say a message is wrong, let us realise that we may have been given inspiration but did not act upon it.

Dedication

As we read and listen to the news, we hear of people with ideals and ambitions who put all their energies into achieving these aims. The ideals are known as causes and their efforts are called dedication which means, whether the causes are right or wrong, by putting their heart and soul into them they become dedicated.

The dictionary says that dedication is 'the putting aside for a set purpose, self-sacrifice, devotion', and it also adds 'devotion to God's cause'. The last definition may be so but not everyone is dedicated to goodness. There are many people in the world today who believe in various causes but whose dedication is anything but godly because it leads to cruelty, inhumanity and even killing or murder. Unfortunately, these people seem to be some of the most dedicated of all but of course there is generally a purpose behind their dedication for they are usually seeking power or wealth and they are not particular as to how they achieve it. These people are so dedicated that they could be called professionals because they hope to get something for their efforts which are certainly not in God's service.

It is similar to those involved with sport who are offered incentives and as soon as this happens the very thought of more wealth seems to bring out the bad side of things in their efforts. Mistakenly, people call these efforts dedication but it is only so in the aspect of being dedicated to wealth.

A lot of people would say that doctors, nurses, priests and clergymen are dedicated and we suppose most of them are but even some can become more interested in power and profit than in their vocation. Today we find they are willing to sell their services to the highest bidder because we all know if we want treatment on the national health service we may have to wait months but if we are willing to pay we can have it next week.

We once asked a dentist why he did work which meant probing into people's mouths. He replied that he was once a doctor but there was more money in being a dentist, so this shows to what cause he was dedicated.

Look back in history and note the clergymen who have manipulated and manoeuvred their followers so that they themselves could benefit. If you read carefully you will notice how the congregations were kept in ignorance so the priests could hold on to their power. As printing and the written word became more popular and, perhaps most important, more available so ignorance faded because people were able to read and think for themselves, thereby diminishing the power of the clergy. Some even became educated and were able to teach others so we had what is known today as lay preachers. These are the ones we would call amateurs because they were not priests and so could not gain power in the church. Eventually they formed breakaway groups which became denominations. These are the ones we would call dedicated.

Modern spiritualism was one of these groups. Small numbers of people, meeting in a sincere way, sought for the truth and became dedicated to that truth. These were dedicated amateurs who fought prejudice, ridicule, and even government, to bring truth to others without any desire for material reward. We are fortunate that they worked so hard for us to worship in peace and comfort because it is not so very long ago that by meeting as we do now we would have been breaking the law. Spiritualism was not recognised as a religion until the early 1950s, so let us not forget those who worked so hard to get us the freedom to worship.

Today there are people who have gifts but will not use them except for their own selfish ends and so cease to be amateurs in an attempt to become professionals: the ones who think more of the fee than the service. It is like the person who created a lot of interest with the suggestion of having a second healing service each week at a particular church until someone said, 'Before we go any further who is going to be here an hour or so before anyone else to get the church ready and warm?' The silence was deafening and so, through lack of dedication, this was one proposal that didn't get off the ground.

The first church that we were involved with was a small hut in which the heating was a coke-burning stove and, before a service could be held, someone had to be there almost two hours beforehand to get the place warm. Now they have a new building where they only have to click a switch to get all the heat and light they want and yet they talk of the sacrifices they have made. We have told them they do not know what sacrifice is because those who founded the church have passed on and none of today's members know where the original church was even situated.

There are so many people who want to be top dogs so that they can bask in the glory and limelight while leaving the work for others to do. This is particularly so when things go wrong but if they were dedicated they would be in a position to prevent that happening.

By being dedicated we draw to ourselves those guides and helpers who are also dedicated and these are the ones who will inspire us in our difficulties. If we are not dedicated we draw to us those who are likeminded because, remember, like attracts like. Therefore let us be dedicated for the sake of those who contact us.

Thoughts

As a man thinketh in his heart so he is. In spiritualism, it is said that thoughts are living things. We also often hear another saying that like attracts like.

When we study these two phrases it behoves us to be very careful how we think, remembering that whatever action we take, it first started out as a thought. We look back in history and shudder at some of the thoughts that must have gone through some people's minds when, in the lust for power and wealth, we consider the actions that have caused wars and bloodshed. What of those who were, and maybe still are, responsible for the deaths and per-secutions of their fellow men in the name of religion? Others have had people stoned and burned to death because they were afraid of them. Afraid because they did not understand the power that these people had within them and did not comprehend how they used that power. Not realising that these people's thoughts must have been spiritual inspiration because of the things they were able to do and predict, as in the story of Jesus Christ. They that sought power did not realise that they possessed the same power as their victims and, if their thoughts had been in the same vein, they would have been able to act in the same way.

In history, however, it has not been all evil thinking because many have shown love and compassion to others by helping and healing when it was needed. We remember, years ago, a young lady reaching the top of her profession and, as the saying goes, the world was her oyster but she turned her back on the fame and fortune that lay before her to go to work with children who were in need.

When we were younger we were 'brought up' in a particular church but eventually we became interested in spiritualism and so we left the original church. Some years later, on a night when it was snowing very hard and there were several inches lying on the ground, someone came knocking at the door. When we went to open it we found a clergyman standing there and we immediately asked him in. Over a cup of tea he told us that he was standing in at the church we had previously attended for a few weeks until he went to take a post in a leper colony in Africa. He had seen our name in the church records and had come along to see why we had not attended church for such a long time. We thanked him for his interest and explained that he was the only one, in eight years, who had bothered to find out why we had not been to church. He had put himself out on a terrible night to come and see us when in fact he could have sat back and taken no notice, letting events drift along until his stint was finished. That leper colony was going to get a wonderful man.

This is what thoughts are all about, or should be, compassion for others, putting one's self out and taking the trouble. Being a Good Samaritan.

We read stories of Jesus healing many people and being followed by thousands who looked upon these things as miracles but again it was the power of thought that enabled these things to be done. His own compassionate thoughts, combined with those who were surrounding him, helped to create a power that enabled spiritual forces to work through him.

Do we realise the power that we have within us and more to the point do we understand what we can achieve with that power? Very often we say that we have ideas or brainwaves when we discover or invent something but have we ever considered where that idea came from in the first place? Could it have been born in the spiritual spheres? Was it spiritual inspiration?

At one time we worked with a gentleman who knew we were interested in spiritualism and so he asked if we could heal his knee which had been troubling him for about three years. We placed our hand on his knee for about two minutes and for a week or so we sent thoughts to him. After this period of time he came to us to tell us his knee was better saying, 'I can run for a bus now.' Following this, things became rather embarrassing because if anyone had an ache or pain this gentleman would tell them to 'see George, he'll cure it'. In passing we would like to say that it was not George who healed him as the next story will illustrate.

When we arrived at work one morning, one of the managers came in and told us his back and shoulders were painful because he had fallen downstairs before leaving home that day. Immediately the familiar words came but the manager did not come to 'see George' although George did send thoughts out to him. However, it was almost six months later before the subject was again broached. The manager came to see George saying, 'I want to tell you something. When I fell downstairs I went to the doctor who told me that there was nothing he could do and I would just have to live with it. Suddenly the pain went so I want to know what you did.' George pointed out that he had not even put a finger on him but he had sent out thoughts so someone else must have healed him. This is the power of thought and this story shows that it is not the healer you can see who is solely responsible for the cure.

We were privileged to hear someone giving an address in which he spoke about a vase of flowers that was on the rostrum saying that, with the power within us, we could create something like a rose. When we have mentioned this to others, even those in spiritualism, we have been met with laughter. However, we understand that in our next phase of life our thoughts will be the only means of communication because we shall not have a physical body that can be used. Therefore if we want a rose, a vase of flowers or even a meal, then we shall only get it through the power of thought.

With thoughts being the only means of communication, it behoves us to be very careful how we think in that life for whilst we are on the earth plane we can think what we like about our neighbour and he cannot hear our thoughts. In the hereafter we have only to think something and it is picked up and understood.

Communications

From the beginning of time man has been able to make himself understood. We recently read an article in a magazine that mentioned the method of sending messages by the beating of drums. It described one historical occasion when news was sent across the length and breadth of Africa at the beginning of this century. Now, although there were many different dialects, this message was understood by everyone and was received long before the news of the happening had been received by conventional means.

Since those early days we have progressed to such things as radio, television, telephones and nowadays we have pictures beamed to us from satellites. We can pick up a telephone, dial a number and in a short time we are speaking to someone who is hundreds of miles away. We understand that at international conferences, where many different languages are spoken, there is an invention that translates the language of the speaker into the various tongues of the listeners. In this way, everyone understands what is being said as it is being spoken.

Truly man has made great strides in material communication but it is a pity that he has not made the same progress in a spiritual sense. He will accept that he can pick up an instrument, put it to his ear and speak to someone who is miles away but tell him his Aunt Mary or Uncle Bill is standing next to him waiting to speak to him and he would say, 'You must be mad, how can they speak to me. They are dead.' If he could only realise they are more alive now than they ever were when they lived on the earth plane. However, if we get him to listen he wants to know how it is done and what the trick is.

One way to explain it is to liken it to radio and television. Man looks upon these things as being marvellous because sounds and pictures can be sent through the air. Yet this is something that spiritual beings have been able to do through thoughts since time began. Now, television and radio sets are very delicate instruments and, as they can be upset by weather and atmospherics, so can different moods or conditions upset our spiritual sets. When a car fitted with a radio passes under a bridge, the broadcast fades out and in a similar way, when we pass through a period of darkness or illness, we lose touch. The helpers are still there but we are in such a fog we cannot get on to their wavelength.

There is a belief that with earthly sets you get a better reception with an aerial and the higher the aerial the stronger the reception. Just before the end of the last war, a group of young men were stationed at a workshop that repaired radio and radar sets. They fitted one of these radios up in their own quarters but the reception was poor until they took a piece of wire around the room. If anyone touched the end of this wire (the aerial) the sound became deafening. Still on this subject of aerials, let us tell you of the man who bought a new television set complete with aerial but the reception was poor. He had the engineers to look at it time after time but there was no improvement, so he wrote to the makers who supplied him with another set, but he still could not get a decent picture. In the meantime the makers stripped the original set, examined it but could find nothing wrong. As the trouble persisted, he decided to try something himself. He collected all the pieces of odd wire he could find, joined them together, hung them out of the bedroom window, plugged the other end into his set and behold the picture was perfect. On examination, it was found that a bolt was missing from the aerial and every time there was a breeze the aerial would sway.

Sometimes when giving or receiving a message, we get into difficulties and cannot put anything in the right place. The message seems to be a jumble of phrases but then a word is spoken, the volume increases and everything falls into place.

Maybe as we sit in circles, each one of us is an insignificant piece of wire and yet when each one of us is joined properly, in love and harmony, what a powerful aerial we make and what a wonderful reception we have. Do not think of ourselves as being of no use but think of the man and his pieces of wire.

When we get to the spirit world we do not want to be like the set that went back to the makers to be examined only to find the verdict to be – 'There is nothing wrong with the set but the aerial needed adjusting and no attempt was made to do so.' If we try to raise our aerials higher, many wonderful things can open before us, things that are similar to apparatus like radar, X-ray and colour television. However, the spirit world does not need to use apparatus to carry out its functions.

Spirit healers do not need to use X-ray machinery to discover what is wrong with a person because they go right to the cause of the trouble immediately. We think colour television is a wonderful invention and yet when we have progressed in a spiritual way, we will be able to see many fantastic things in colours we never knew existed, so let us get our spiritual radar working and we will be able to pierce the fogs, mists and gloom.

The Power of Prophecy

We are always reading the words that are placed on what is known as 'the wayside pulpit' and we saw some recently that were advertising a church service with the words, 'The Power of Prophecy'. We suppose that this particular church's idea of prophecy is very different to ours.

The dictionary says that prophecy is a prediction: the prediction of future events and the interpretations of the Scriptures. A prophet is 'one who prophesies' and one who is spiritually inspired'.

We supposed the definition of interpreting the Scriptures applies to the church where we saw the notice but in fact it applies to all churches because everyone can make out a case for their beliefs. We can all take quotations from whatever Scriptures we read and make them fit our beliefs.

At a funeral service we attended, the clergyman conducting the service read some words from the Book of Isaiah that prophesied the coming of Jesus Christ so because of this, and the fact that Jesus was going to be crucified, God would abolish death. We would pose the question 'What about the people who lived and died before these words were written?' Are they condemned? Our Scriptures tell us that there is no such thing as death but of course the clergyman had not read them in the way that we had done.

In our opinion, the best prophets are those who cannot read because their minds are not then coloured by other people's beliefs and they cannot interpret Scriptures that they cannot read. Look at the holy men of the East, they are hermits, living alone, not mixing with others but what prophets they are. There is a story of someone going to see one of these men who was greeted with the words, 'It has taken you a long time to come' and at his look of amazement the seer said, 'Yes, my son, I knew you were coming even before you had made up your mind.'

What about children, those who cannot read? There was one child whose mother was in hospital with circulation trouble and who had already lost part of her toe through amputation. On one of the visits, the family were told that there was a possibility that she could lose her leg, so you can imagine what the journey home that night was like. Suddenly, the little girl burst out with the words, 'I don't know what the matter is with you all and can't understand what you are crying about. She has not lost her leg yet.' When that mother died she had lost part of her foot but she still had both legs.

Then there was the little child of four years whose mother bought her a pair of shoes but she would not wear them. The child had told her mother that she was saving them for her holidays but as the mother was pregnant they could not afford a holiday. The reason we had visited them that evening was to tell them that we had booked a flat at the seaside and, as it catered for five, we wondered whether they would like to come with us. After all it was not going to cost any more for five people than for two. They came with us so the child was right but the amazing thing was that we could not get her to take off her shoes, not even on the sands. The same little girl told everyone that she was going to have a little 'bruvver' and, although her mother told her it could be a sister, she insisted that it would be a brother. Lo and behold when the baby arrived it was a boy.

Where did these children get their information when they could not read? The only conclusion we can come to is that they were divinely inspired or, rather, spiritually inspired. These happenings confirm a belief that we have had for a long time of the truth that for the first few years of our lives we are nearer to the spirit world than at any time we are on earth. Therefore we are not surprised that children are such good prophets but feel it is a pity they are not allowed to develop their natural gifts.

Prophecy is given to us in many ways, such as in dreams, and if we consider or try to interpret them we will find we are being guided. We have ideas or brainwaves but surely these are spiritually inspired? We were once privileged to see a psychic artist at work. His opening words were, 'Some mediums stand in front of you, point and say I can see such and such with you', but I cannot work in that manner.' However, he must have spiritually inspired because he gave more than prophecy, he gave proof of life after death through his sketches.

We are all spiritually inspired and we should go back to our childhood to develop these gifts because it makes one wonder what Jesus meant when he said, 'Unless ye become as one of these.' If we adopt a childlike approach to spiritual things we would not need mediums to stand in front of us to give us proof because we could receive our own and, more important, we would understand the 'fuller life'.

What Is It All About?

Why do we go to church and why is it a particular church? There are dozens of churches, so why pick one specially? What reason is there to go to a spiritualist church and, when we go, do we know what it is all about?

Some time ago we gave a message to a young man who accepted it without question but after the service he came to speak to us explaining that he was a newcomer and he had received two or three messages similar to the one we had given to him. He then came out with the question, 'What is it all about?'

At another service, we stood to sing the closing hymn and, for the first time that evening, we noticed a young man standing towards the back of the church. Although we had not been aware of him throughout the service, we were immediately drawn to him. As the service ended, we went to speak with him. His first words were, 'I have been weighing you up and I don't know whether you are a fake, a fluke or genuine.'

We explained to him that we were answering a call for help because the original medium who had been booked could not attend. It was a miserable foggy night and I could have been sitting at home reading a good book or watching television in front of a nice fire. Furthermore, as we were receiving no material gain, there was no reason whatever to fake anything and as for being a fluke or being lucky in our efforts, it was not saying much for those spirit guides who came to help us.

This young man was making the same mistake as many others when they see a medium working, by thinking the medium is the most important person and that he or she is doing it all themselves. They think the mediums are the be-all and end-all and that they possess supernatural powers when there is nothing supernatural about them. We would liken the experience to a child listening to someone reading from a book, because to the child who cannot read, the person who is doing the reading is someone who is clever and who is something special. Eventually the child learns to read and so it becomes a natural thing. So one thing that it is all about is the realisation that these things are as natural as learning how to read.

Being of nature, there are laws and regulations to be observed and those who are sincere are aware of this because they know that if you interfere with nature then you are in trouble. If we try to fake or fluke these gifts, if we start abusing them, we shall soon be found out for what we are. These gifts are truly pearls beyond price and there is a lot more to them than just the use of giving and receiving of messages. Not everyone has the knowledge of these gifts or the value of them but, when the realisation comes that they are a natural part of life, we can start developing them in a similar way to our material gifts.

Now to some of us education can be a bore, a bind or even a waste of time and yet when we have received it no one can take it from us. Give someone a fortune and in six months they could have lost every penny of it but give them knowledge and they have it for the rest of their lives. No one can ever take away our spiritual gifts, even if we never use them whilst on earth because we brought them with us and we take them back with us. If we progress in a spiritual way on earth we have a sensation of being raised above material worries (words cannot describe the feeling) and no one can ever take this sensation away from us. It is something money cannot buy, riches beyond price, and so this is something else that it is all about.

When we are asked what we must do with these riches, we answer that we should share all our wealth, whether material or spiritual, so that others can have help and assistance, for we believe this is why they are given to us. If we cast our bread upon the waters, it will be returned in increasing measure, especially spiritually.

There are so many people who are in need of healing physically, mentally and spiritually that this is where we can help but we must not expect to receive material riches for doing so and, if we are sincere in our efforts, we would not seek them.

People say to us, 'If you can do and see these things why can't you win yourself a fortune. You help others so why can't you receive something in return?' We do get something back because I think I can honestly say that I have not wanted for anything as I have never been in the gutter, although I have been on the edge of it. Every one receives something and this again is what it's all about. We ask God and the spirit friends for help and then worry whether we are going to receive it or more to the point whether we shall get it in the way we want it. As we progress, we learn to develop the patience to wait for events to take place and more important to accept them whether they are as we planned or not.

Here are two examples. We wrote after a job but when the day of the interview arrived we had changed our mind. Someone from the company came to see us, however, and told us it was in our interests to go for the interview. We went to the company, had an interview and it was one of the best moves we had ever made. On another occasion, a young man in business wanted to do some trading with a company in the city but could not find them at the address he had been given, nor at the second or the third but, after spending most of the day looking, he found them. After talking to them he discovered it was not in his interests to pursue the matter. This young man was receiving guidance but did not realise it because by not finding the persons he wanted, after three attempts, he should have realised that he was being told not to bother.

This is something we gain by trying to discover 'what it is all about'.

How Is It Done?

Have you ever realised that sometimes in a matter of days certain events take place independently of each other and yet they can all be related to a certain theme?

Sometime ago we went to take a service at a church which was some distance from home and therefore we started a little earlier than we need have done in case there were any mishaps on the way. This meant that, because we had a trouble-free journey, we arrived half an hour too soon. However, when we tried the doors we found the church was closed and, as we had been in difficulties with this church over bookings on previous occasions, we began to wonder what had gone wrong. We sat there for about twenty minutes before someone came along, tried the door and walked on up the road but eventually came back and opened the doors. At this we walked over and the lady asked if we were with them that evening. We replied that we hoped so but we also asked what time the service started and when she said 'six-thirty', we said that we were cutting it a bit fine.

Other people came in and the service started about ten minutes late. We must state at this point that the church had been prepared for decorating and because of this the carpets had been taken up which meant that the floorboards were showing. We had sung the opening hymn and were some way into the prayer, when there was a commotion at the door and some people started to walk down the church, bare boards and all. You can imagine the noise that six pairs of feet made as they walked down to the front row. It was such that we had to stop midway through the prayer. Most people would say that this was not the best of starts to a divine service but those six actually made the service. The six were two children, two teenagers and two older people.

We gave the address and then came to the clairvoyance during which we gave the older lady some proof but it was when we spoke to the young man that something astonishing happened. We asked him if he knew the name Peter and did he know someone who went to train for the priesthood to which he replied, 'No'. The older lady said, 'He doesn't but I do and I would like you to tell me how you know these things?' After the service she said that when her mother was young she moved down from the north to be in service with a family who had a son named Peter who had gone into the priesthood. She herself was not even born then so it was impossible for the young man to know anything about it. She then asked, 'How is it done?'

Just after this we were sitting in the congregation at church when a lady began to talk about her husband's attitude to clairvoyance. He wanted to know how we knew that these messages came from departed souls and we asked – if not, where did they come from, but there was no answer to that. The lady also spoke of her son who had university degrees and she said that he would tear to shreds any argument that could be put forward. When the service started the first hymn was about Samuel's ear, mind and faith. The last line of this hymn reads 'truths that are hidden from the wise' and we pointed out to the lady that the answer to her son was in those words.

A few days after this, we were watching a service on television in which the clergyman told a story of Jews who were imprisoned in Germany during the war. One of them wrote on the wall of his cell, 'I believe the sun is shining although I cannot see it behind the clouds, I know that God is there although I cannot see him.'

We could say we believe in our spiritual friends and the guidance they bring because, even if we cannot see them, we can sense them. Not everyone will accept these things because if they cannot explain them scientifically then they do not exist.

Now to answer the first lady's question. We would tell her that when someone dies their soul or spirit lives on and goes back to where it came from originally. The only part of us which dies is our physical body, the part that we can see and the part that was made by our parents. God gave us the other and it is the only part that goes back. This world we live in is a solid one but the one we go back to is very different. It is a world of thought, of emotion, where there is no need to use our tongue, voice box, words or speech to communicate because, as soon as we think something, it will be picked up and understood.

When the question is asked how do the mediums know these things the honest answer is that they don't but remember that the medium, mostly through the power of thought from the congregation, is able to lift him or herself towards this lighter and brighter world. At the same time, those from this other world come to make contact with the medium so in fact it is teamwork, from the medium, the guides and also the congregation.

As the medium and spirit friends make contact so the medium comes close to that thought world and is able to pick up the thoughts that are being sent through the atmosphere in a similar way that radio waves and television pictures are sent. This is the way in which some people who would not consider themselves as mediums sometimes get premonitions. However, back to the medium who gets someone close to the person he or she has to speak to and, through spiritually inspired thoughts, is able to give evidence to that person.

Everyone has this ability to reach outwards and upwards to this thought world. Because we are called spiritualists and meet in a spiritualist church, do not think we are privileged or are some sort of chosen people. We can call ourselves what we like but let us remember that everyone brings this power and ability with them when they enter this world. A lot of people have a fear of gypsies because they think they possess some supernatural power or some gift that is looked upon as uncanny. There is nothing uncanny or supernatural about them: they are merely exercising a natural law.

Oh, if only the doctors, the specialists and scientists could or would raise their thoughts to this so-called supernatural power, what wonderful results could be achieved! Just think how great it would be if they could lift themselves so high and become so inspired that there would be no need for them to cut and carve people to cure them. If, by looking at people they could see that there was something wrong with them, they would be able to heal them without resorting to surgery.

Give a thought to what could happen if the world's leaders in their differing spheres recognised and tried to develop this power that they have within them. There could be peace, plenty and a sharing of God's and nature's gifts.

Creation Not Evolution

We bring you some words that we read from a poster advertising a religious meeting: 'Creation Not Evolution'. Although we did not know what the intended meaning of that phrase was, it made us think.

Evolution is to change, to unfold, to develop and to progress. Our belief is that if there is creation then there must be evolution because creation, whatever it is, starts as a thought and even the thought itself is evolution. Let us explain this by saying when we have a thought, an idea or a brainwave, we like to think it is ours but who put it into our head in the first place? We read through the history of those who have invented or discovered something but of all the discoveries and inventions we read about have we ever thought they may have started as inspiration in the spirit world? So what about our thought, where did it begin and was it already evolving when it reached us?

Anyway, we decide to do something with our idea and so we use our hands to create something which can be seen because it is solid for, after all, we cannot see a thought. When we look at this creation we are looking at the result of evolution, thus proving that there is such a thing.

This is a solid world in which we live and we are told that everything is made of atoms and atoms consist of things called protons and electrons. Everything we can think of – wood, steel, cloth, stone, earth, the vegetable world and even ourselves – is made of atoms. To understand this truth, let us take a simple illustration to show what evolution is and how it works. Let us take the chair you are sitting on and examine how it developed. A long time ago, a seed dropped from a tree into the soil and again, after a period of time, with the help of nature, a tree grew from that seed. Later, someone in the timber business came along seeking suitable trees and chose the tree grown from that seed. He took it away, cut it into suitable lengths and then someone came along to buy some of the timber to make some chairs, including the one you are sitting on. No longer it is called a seed, a tree or timber, because it is shaped like a chair, but the basic things are the same. Whatever it is called we still have atoms making up the finished article.

There comes a time when the chair has served its usefulness, so it is thrown on to the bonfire to be burned and all we have left is a pile of ashes. We hear you saying, 'Now that it is a pile of ashes that must surely be the end', but it is not because those ashes are still atoms, protons and electrons. Perhaps not so many of one and maybe more of the other but nevertheless atoms are still there in a different form.

Nothing in this world ever stands still and we have only to look back through our lives to see the changes that have taken place, the developments we have experienced, although at the time we were possibly puzzled by the changes. Personally we can think of one part of our evolution where we suffered badly in a material sense and yet because of, or in spite of this, we later realised that we had progressed spiritually. Perhaps the atoms had changed shape.

As we enter this world, we are similar to the seed that fell from the tree and, as the tree grew from that seed, so our evolution took, and still is taking, place. As mankind progressed, so there was advancement in other areas, such as improvement in working conditions, the abolishment of slavery and new thinking in religions.

Having already stated that nothing ever stands still, we must ask where are we going from here? Is our shape going to change? Is our outlook, our thought in a similar way to St Paul's, going to change? Change we shall have to even if it is after we are burned or buried because we cannot stop evolution and, as life is everlasting, we shall just keep evolving.

2
Primary Lessons

Doctrine

You may have heard us, as we pray, ask for those who have power and authority to receive spiritual inspiration so that they use that power in a way that will benefit their fellow men, for power can be used in so many other ways. When we pray for those who have authority, we are asking for religious leaders, church officials, politicians, industrialists, union leaders, those having charge of younger ones and anyone involved with hospitals or institutions. We begin like this because of some words that we read – 'the importance of doctrine'.

What is doctrine? That which is taught by a person, a school or church, a particular truth, a special dogma, a principle of belief or creed. The word doctrinaire means the application of principle with no allowance for circumstances or, in straightforward language, obstinacy.

Shall we consider the troubles of the world and see how much of it is due to doctrine and obstinacy? Take industry, where we find management on one side who have been brought up to believe one doctrine but on the other we have the workforce, represented by the unions, who read and follow the doctrine according to *their* gospel. We are not going to judge who is right or wrong but one thing we are certain of is that by being so doctrinaire they do not help matters. We find the same thing in the political arena where one doctrine is fighting another with the result that someone who is innocent suffers.

What about the differing doctrines in the various nations throughout the world where certain people's philosophy is to impose their will on to others, so trying to force their way of thinking on to them and not being particular how they do it? If anyone criticises, they are told it is being done in the name of patriotism, which leads to the question, is patriotism a good thing? But that is another story.

Unfortunately, doctrine and being doctrinaire appears to be more prevalent in religions than anywhere else, with people even knocking on our doors expounding their beliefs by quoting from the Bible and giving their interpretation of it.

At one time we had a shop adjacent to a church and school of a certain belief and the children used to come and inform us that their religion was better than any other. They too could quote passages and references to make their point which, to us, denoted that they had been tutored, or even brainwashed, to have the answers so ready to hand. We should learn from these experiences because we should not become so doctrinaire that we cannot appreciate other people's points of view for, was it not said, 'Other sheep I have which are not of this fold'? Our thoughts should not come from the head but rather the heart so that we can advertise our spirituality through our actions and deeds, not by words issuing from our mouths.

We were talking to a young man about cars and we mentioned that we used ours mostly for something that we were interested in and which gave us a lot of pleasure. As we talked on a little longer he said, 'You seem reluctant to discuss this interest', so we told him that if we thought he would be interested in the subject we were willing to talk all night, but when we mentioned it was of a spiritual nature the conversation died. He did not seem to realise that we could have talked all night but at the end he would be bored to death.

This reminds us of a letter in a newspaper which said the church should take an interest and action in industrial matters. We do not think that this is a good thing when we consider some of the damage the church has done by sending missionaries to so-called backward countries. There was too much preaching and not enough practising and we feel it could be the same with industry.

Let our doctrine be one of love or, at least, tolerance and let others follow our example, not our words. Let us be truthful because, if we cannot show love, how can we tell others what it is? Some doctrines create fear but you cannot reap a harvest of love by sowing seeds of fear. Therefore let us put into practice the principle that is spoken of throughout the world but which is not very often used – let us practise not preach the brotherhood of man.

Principles

Some time ago we read a report about a television programme in which a man had been interviewed and, during the questioning, he had said something like 'no man who has principles can ever be a leader'.

What is a principle? A fundamental truth, a moral rule, uprightness. Each day of our lives we can pick up our newspapers and read of people who have tried to be leaders but have failed, not because they have had principles but rather the lack of them. To put it in modern language, they have tried to fiddle, bamboozle and trick others until they have committed the biggest error of all by being 'found out'.

None of us can be proud of the lack of principles we show from time to time even in things that we feel are of little consequence: receiving too much change in a shop and saying nothing about it; of being persistently late for work; of not pulling our weight when we are at work; of getting a position of authority and abusing it by not using the authority in the proper way. We knew a gentleman who at one time had worked in coal mines until he attained the position of overseer. Part of his responsibility was to make sure that the safety precautions were adhered to. This meant that at times the miners were slowed down or even stopped in their work, thereby losing money. Of course this produced a lot of moaning and groaning, even though the regulations were for their own benefit. However, the man's boss told him, 'The more they moan the more convinced I am that you are doing your job right.' That man could have taken the line of least resistance but he didn't because he had principles.

Sometime ago there were a number of letters in the local paper about well-known people taking part in religious services. One clergyman said he asked them to his services because they drew the crowds and the money. You notice there is no mention of spiritual welfare or the work that the church is supposed to be doing. We do not hear of the 'founders' of religions stooping so low as to perpetrate such tricks and we do not suppose people like Mother Teresa think about what is in it for herself.

There is nowhere in the Bible where it is shown that Jesus put more emphasis on the material than the spiritual things of life. He need only to look at a person, for his whole being to change in such a way that he would follow him. This is the way he chose his disciples because, when he said, 'Come follow me', that is what they did. He could, by looking at a person, lift him out of this world and make him search his conscience. Remember the tax collector who hid in a tree and was told to come down as Jesus wished to dine with him. What a meal that must have been. He was a changed man after it, so perhaps he discovered some principles he thought he had lost.

Now, when we come to discuss spirituality, we would say that if we have principles in a material way then we are half way to having them spiritually. Perhaps we show a desire to sit in a developing circle but, after being accepted, we show no desire to make progress and so we are in the similar position to not giving of our best when we are at work.

Our experience is that when we try to bring principles into spiritual development we get a lot of excuses about why certain sitters cannot do this or do that. Insist that the circle begins at the appointed time, that the sitters attend each week (if not a very good excuse must be produced), but above all every sitter must take his or her turn in opening and closing the circle with a prayer. Some people will say but you cannot place these conditions on the sitters and our answer to that is, 'if they cannot accept these rules then there is no place in the circle for them'. This is a principle and by applying it, we are sorting out the wheat from the chaff and discovering the genuine ones because, after all, the circle is not a place for just receiving messages.

Now most of us lose financially when we are late or absent from work, so what do we lose by acting in a similar way spiritually? We lose the confidence of our spirit friends and rightly so because we cannot expect them to guide and help us only when we need them. Let us realise one important truth, which is that the guides come to help us because they too want to progress and this is one way they can achieve that aim. If we are not going to be reliable, then we are going to attract guides who are of a similar nature. There could come a time when we need them and discover they are not there.

Of course this applies more so to mediums who do public work and so it is important for them to have principles. We were once told by a medium of many years' experience in public work that, if we were stuck when giving clairvoyance and could not 'get anything home', to make some remark and leave the person to whom we were talking. To us this shows a lack of principle and we must remember there could come a time when we are left stranded in mid-air because the guide has adopted the same attitude.

Before we finish with principles, we must say something about mediums' fees because some people think mediums should work for nothing and even tell the medium that Jesus Christ did not accept a fee. Maybe he didn't but he was cared for by his friends. We are not against mediums accepting fees providing they recognise that the service is more important than the reward. In fact the service should be paramount to everything else and the reward that the mediums should be looking for is that they have done a good job. At the conclusion of their service, they should feel on top of the world.

Challenges

A challenge is a call, a summons to fight, to defy, to dare, to invite to a contest. Everyone of us has to face challenges of one sort or another during our lives. Maybe it is a summons from someone who is sending out a call for help and this could mean having to do something we would rather not do, like giving bad news. We have to speak our mind about injustices and are not always liked for it. When we lose a loved one, we are facing the challenge of perhaps having to face the future alone. Isn't it a challenge when we ourselves are called from this earth? The very fact that we are here on the earth plane is proof that we have already faced one challenge.

We once heard the phrase; 'it is peaceful in paradise.' Of course it is but we cannot expect to be protected all the time, so it was put to us 'Are you going to stay in the Garden of Eden for ever, or do you intend to go to the earth plane so that you can mix some of the rough soil with the finer variety of paradise?' Because we don a spiritual body when we come to earth, it is the material challenges that seem to affect us the most. This material body in itself offers a challenge because we are still spiritual beings and therefore we should face spiritual challenges, because one day we have to go back to Eden.

Every missed opportunity or avoided challenge is a scar on our spiritual advancement and we feel that this is a pity because there are people who have spiritual gifts but do not use them to help others. When we were asked why we did spiritual work, we answered that we believed that wealth, in whatever form it is, should be shared and therein lies the challenge. It is no good an artist painting beautiful pictures if they are going to be left in a cellar where no one can see them, or a musician playing wonderful music if no one can hear it.

We know someone who is fortunate enough to be able to see things clairvoyantly in a way as natural as others see things through their physical eyes. It may be a strange thing to say but this young man will not try to develop this gift further by discovering what these visions mean. He will not accept the challenge and the discipline of working with the guides. It is all right giving someone a

message by telling them what you can see but it is not enough
because we must also give them proof, after all that is the basis of
spiritualism, fact rather than faith.

If we receive a message without proof then we must challenge
the medium and the guides by examining that message over and
over again and if we are not satisfied then we must dismiss it. But
we must not dismiss it because it is not what we want to know.
Remember, we receive what we need not what we want. Jesus
Christ faced a challenge, like the rest of us, by coming to earth and
he faced another one by being tempted to use his gifts for material
gain but that was not the reason for his coming. He did not come
to found a religion and we feel that none of the other religious
leaders did either. They came to bring new thoughts and to demonstrate the spiritual way of life.

Take a man like Buddha, who was born into a rich family and
could have sat back to enjoy material wealth but no, like Jesus, he
was not satisfied with the conditions around him and so he decided
to do something about it. Both Buddha and Jesus felt and taught
compassion and love to their fellow men, thus facing the challenge.

We must recognise that these leaders were more prophets than
priests but today's religious leaders are different because they
belong to what is known as 'the establishment' and therefore have
to follow the dictates, decrees and dogmas set out by the establishment. The prophets did not belong to any such organisation and
so what they said or did came from within, from their hearts. It
was sincere.

Where today is there one religious leader who will face today's
challenges and will fight against stupidity, cruelty, wickedness or
indifference? Who is going to challenge the blood lust of a man
who is fighting his brother, very often in the name of religion? Who
is going to do something about the greed of man who causes prices
to rise, thus creating shortages and even starvation? Where is the
leader who is going to lead? We ask this not only of religions but
also of individual churches, of nations and of both sides of industry.
No one seems to want to know as long as they have the power,
the glory and, in some cases, the riches that go with them. The
responsibility they do not want. If only they would use their authority, how much better the world would be. If they set the right
example we may even have others following it.

What about us? Are we willing to face challenges, are we ready
to make sacrifices or do we want to sit back and let the world
go by? Shall we attain important positions, sit back and not take
responsibility?

We know we can get weary of well-doing and feel like packing it all in but when we get like this we must realise that this is another challenge, so what about facing up to it? If we don't do it now, we shall have to later.

Publicity

Today spiritualism and all things psychic have been receiving a lot of publicity through articles in newspapers, magazines and programmes on radio or television. The writers and presenters mention the words 'supernatural', 'supernormal' and 'paranormal' but rarely mention 'spiritualism'.

What we would like to ask is, 'Does this publicity show spiritualism in a good light and, if so, are we taking advantage of it?' Most of the publicity has been about the phenomena of being able to contact the so-called dead and receive messages from them. They have it all wrong, however, because no one on this earth can contact the dead: it is the spirits of those who are called dead who contact *us*.

This is why when we read a newspaper report of a well-known medium and clairvoyant we were rather put out. In the article she is said to have been in contact with some very well known people and at the end she is reported as saying, 'Now who else would you like me to bring back?' If this statement is true then it is very bad publicity because she should know that she cannot demand any one to come back. No one can ask for their Uncle Bill or Auntie Mary to return if Auntie or Uncle have no wish to do so. People see these reports and, not understanding them, say that they are supernatural or supernormal. This infers that they are above the laws of nature or outside the natural law. When we consider this definition we should realise that it cannot be feasible because nothing and no one can be outside or above the natural law.

After one television programme we were caught up in a discussion with two workmates and besides talking about the programme we gave them instances of phenomena that we knew of. One of these had been reported in the newspapers and one chap said that he had read about them. We told them that the story was quite true because we knew the family concerned. This family were all well educated, financially comfortable so there was no need for them to tell fairy stories. Added to this was the fact that this young man had been investigated by researchers to see if he was genuine. After listening to this, the second fellow said, 'I am not calling you a liar but you must admit it takes a bit of swallowing.'

My wife had been in hospital for a serious operation and one day after coming home she was not feeling at all well so she went for a lie-down. Whilst resting she sent out thoughts for healing and was amazed to feel all sorts of activity in her stomach, so that she has always been convinced that someone was bringing her comfort. Would any one swallow that?

These things they call supernatural. There is nothing *more* natural but how do we explain them to others? How many, watching and listening to the programmes or reading the magazines, were able to swallow that which they have seen, heard or read? How many of them have changed their lives because of these things?

Has going to a spiritualist church changed your way of life? The *way of life*, isn't that what we should be talking about? Not the ability to give and receive messages from those in the further life. Has sitting in a developing circle had any effect on your thoughts and ideals? We have had many experiences with circles, including quite a few disappointments besides upliftments.

A lady, who had attended spiritualist churches for many years, asked if she could join the circle we were conducting at the time and, after much thought, we agreed that she could. Week after week this lady would 'give off' messages. We decided to remind not only her but the other sitters of something they may have forgotten. We reminded them all that giving messages was all right but before the message we must give proof, such as names, birthdays, physical conditions and so on, for the recipients to know who the message came from. The lady did not like it and said, 'If you have faith in your guides they will give you the message.' We replied, 'If you have faith in your guides they will give you the proof.' That lady did not come to the circle again.

Another lady who had sat with us for quite a time and had also sat in other circles disappointed us because after one circle we were having a chat and the conversation turned to the unemployed. This lady said that she had no sympathy for them and why should she worry about what happened to her neighbours. This attitude sickened and saddened us because it appeared that during the time she had been sitting with us she had learned nothing or perhaps we had taught her nothing. Perhaps she thought the circles were only for developing clairvoyance and not for such things as the brotherhood of man.

No wonder Jesus said, 'I have been with you so long and still you do not understand.' Although people consider the things that Jesus did as miracles he brought a deeper message and this message was 'love thy neighbour'.

So remembering this, if by any chance we are interviewed, we will be able to say that spiritualism has taught us spirituality and by learning that, we have love and compassion for our fellow men. That we are here for an education – the progression of the soul which begins here and now and not in some far distant place in the future. When we say this let us be able to say it in truth and sincerity.

Power and Authority

When we look around the world today we see men seeking power; we see those who have power desperately trying to hang on to it and we see others, who should be leading, being led themselves.

What is this thing called power and, going a little further, what is authority because although we may think they are both the same there could be a difference? So we read that power means to have the right to govern, to hold sway, to have influence, to have influence over someone or something and, lastly, it means energy. Now authority is said to be 'legal or genuine power' and again we have the words 'sway and influence' but we also have the words 'the right'. It also implies a group of people. The phrases 'to hold sway' and 'to have influence' give the impression that the definition means to 'lord it over someone'.

By what means do these people get this power? It could be by education, by passing examinations, by promotion, by being chosen or voted in or through the more sinister ways of force, bloodshed and trickery. How about the use of this power when they have it? If they are ambitious in a personal way they will certainly use it to get what they want, even if it means trampling over others to achieve their ends.

When we talk of these people, the leaders or perhaps we should say those who have authority over others, we speak of those who have power over nations, those with power throughout industry, in religions and churches. During our everyday lives we see various instances of how this power is used or misused and we can think of one young man, who through promotion was pushed higher and higher. He used the power this gave him to the point of being rude and having bad manners to such an extent that those who worked with and for him asked higher management to speak to him about his attitude. Because of this, things became a little better but, although this young man had made material progress, he lost a few friends by doing so. We can see similar things happening in all walks of life.

Let us look at industry in its broader sense and when we say that we are speaking of both sides – management and workers. We all know of dirty tricks, broken promises and most of all of the

evasion of the issues by not making decisions, leaving it for someone else to take the blame. We have known meetings to take place
to discuss some problem where, after talking for two or three hours,
the decision that was arrived at was, 'We will have another meeting
at a later date'. All this because no one had the strength to say yes
or no. We have known people in authority abusing their power
and at the same time punishing another person for doing the same
thing.

Similarly, we have the same thing between nations, when the
leaders try to score points off each other by ranting and raving
against each other and then expecting the same people to sit around
a table to discuss peace. How many times has a large nation taken
action against a smaller one when trying to impose its will but, if
another large nation is involved, then a blind eye is turned on the
dispute.

Unfortunately, we have problems of power and authority in
churches and religions where the followers are ordered, or at least
expected, to obey certain instructions, dogmas or creeds so that they
are not allowed to think for themselves. However, when someone in
authority tries to bring new thinking to the people, he is criticised
or even ridiculed. Like the new Bishop of Durham, Dr Jenkins,
when he spoke in a television interview just after his induction. He
cast doubts on the Immaculate Conception and the occurrence of
miracles both 2,000 years ago and today. Of course the same thing
occurs when the clergy speak of spiritualism or psychic gifts
because they know these things exist but prefer to ignore them.

As with religion, so it is with individual churches, when someone
has attained a position and because of this expects everyone else
to follow whatever he says. We are sorry to say that this happens
in spiritualist churches. People in power have this position and
intend to hang on to it by hook or crook, not wishing to hear others'
ideas or points of view. They do not want the younger ones to play
an active part in the running of the church and we have even
known annual general meetings where members have been told
who to vote for so that certain individuals are kept off the commit-
tee. Because of these attitudes in every field we have leaders who
will not, cannot, or are frightened to, take decisions.

Of course, something like this happened two thousand years ago
when a group of men had power and were desperately trying to
hang on to it, especially when a man came along with a new
message, a new teaching which drew crowds to him. Because of
this ability to draw the people to him, the rulers contrived to have
him put to death. They did not understand the message he brought

or the power within him because they had never seen or heard anything like it before.

What about the power we have within us? Have we recognised it? Do we know how to use it? Let us remember it was given to us to help others and not for our own benefit or ego like some of those we have mentioned. In our small way we could have something within us that may be of help to others and, if we pass it on then that something, that power, will become stronger. There was a man whose hands used to perspire a lot but he did not realise that he had healing power. How many more are like that man?

We read the story of Jesus taking some of his disciples up the mountainside where they immediately fell asleep, a deep sleep. Or did they? Could it be that they were so overcome with spiritual power that they went into a trance which created ectoplasm that enabled spiritual beings to speak with Jesus? Again it is said that we can do greater things than these, but do we try? Man with all his education does not seem to be interested.

Looking back through history we can see how man has progressed from firelight to oil lamps, to gaslight, to electricity, so that at the flick of a switch we have light. Spiritually, man has not progressed any further than the firelight.

When we experience power failure in a material sense a lot of folks are lost because they cannot cope in the dark. Spiritually we could be in the same predicament, not because of a breakdown but because we do not know how to switch on. When we receive material power we have to pay for it but spiritual power is given to us and should be considered a privilege. This poses the question – is it too cheap? Remember, it is the most precious thing we have, so let us use it.

Patriotism – Good or Bad?

We all have a family even if that family is in-laws related to us only by marriage. We mention the last half of that sentence because we once knew a young lady who, until she married, had no living relative and was truly an orphan. Being a member of a family we suppose we do our best to benefit that family and rescue or defend any member who is in trouble.

Which is the best way to do this? Do we make excuses for them when they are in trouble or do they receive what is known as a short, sharp lesson? Let us look at one or two examples.

Firstly, there was the lady whose son was always in trouble with the police but all she said or did was, 'He is a good lad really but it is the company he keeps.' We wonder if she ever did anything to change that company. What of the parents who say, 'He or she has had a good home and a good education so we cannot understand the way he or she has developed.' Could it be that the child was given too much of the material things of life and not enough love and discipline, thus becoming spoilt?

Consider the story of the mother who reported her son to the police because he had stolen a small amount of money from her. To her neighbours this mother was wicked and a traitor but she said that if he was not stopped her son would become a criminal. He was put in a home for three weeks while inquiries were made about his character. During this period of detention he had time to reflect and he decided that he was going down the wrong pathway. Compare these stories and decide who showed the most loyalty to their family.

Now on to other groups of people who could be likened to families but who we call communities. We went to take a service at a church which was about twelve-miles distant from home and yet in that short distance the dialect changed enormously. There were people at this church who we had seen at a place six miles nearer home and even their 'twang' was different. We can recall sitting in the waiting room of the railway station at Newcastle upon Tyne listening to two men who were speaking to each other across the room. We would challenge anyone who was not born in the area to translate what they were saying because we could not understand a word of it. Apart from differing dialects, these communities have differing ways of life, even to the extent of eating what seem to us strange foods.

Let us move on to the wider spheres of the various nations of the world. Each nation, like the local communities, has its own culture, its own type of government, its own special trades or industries and its own beliefs or religions. To us these things may be strange but that does not necessarily mean that they are wrong. Because we do not understand their language, it does not mean that we should not try to communicate with them.

We do not think that it is any mischance or accident that most of the European countries now have an influx of immigrants many of whom have children who were born in their adopted country. We have hope especially that from these young ones, there is going to be a better understanding of the various cultures. We have a nephew, who when in his teens was very friendly with a Jamaican boy and his family, so much so that they visited each others homes for meals. In those days it was, to say the least, uncommon for races to mix in this manner but we hope that in the future this will become more usual.

Today we hear people say shall we have an Indian or Chinese and the thing they are talking about is a meal that years ago would have been a novelty. Today people look upon visiting a 'foreign' restaurant as a standard part of life. If we can accept their cooking and meals, why cannot we at least tolerate other parts of their culture? Oh yes we, know people say 'but they will not accept ours' and we appreciate this but two wrongs do not make a right.

Shall we move on to an area that has no barriers or boundaries and stretches from one country across into another? This area is religion and it has caused more argument, more hatred and possibly more bloodshed than any other area we can think of. All religions need bringing up to date, need revitalising and need new ideas to achieve this, but when someone tries to do something about it he is immediately shot down.

We have a bishop of the Church of England who has tried to bring new sense and thoughts to some of the old stories of the Bible but all he received for his efforts was ridicule and contempt.

All of us are guilty of what we would call negative thinking in relation to other religions and if thoughts are living things then we could all be guilty of something deeper. Guilty of setting in motion evolution of hateful thoughts which could build into something that is much worse. Let us remember that the thought is father to the action. It is to be found in spiritualism and we also realise that many spiritualists think they are a race apart, a chosen race. We do not understand why because if we study other religions we will find that there is much that is aligned to our beliefs. Everyone, and we mean everyone, both them and us, must make the effort to be more tolerant of one another.

Everyone must try to understand the dialects of people in other districts and we feel that the younger ones of today are trying to do this because they are not so reserved and mix more easily than their elders. Look at the peace movements, not only in this country but throughout the world, and we will find they are made up mostly of young people. At one time they were considered a joke but not any more.

Maybe we are only small cogs in a big wheel but let us think peace for if we get peace in our minds then we shall know what peace is. Some folks pray for peace not knowing what it is. Build up peace in our family and it could spread to the local community and beyond. Do this by biting our tongues when we feel like saying something that could cause hurt, anger or humiliation.

When we go to the spirit world, heaven or whatever we like to call it, we shall find that all cultures will have to be accepted for the benefit of all because there will be no special areas for Roman Catholics, Buddhists, Muslims or spiritualists. Another thing, we will not see black, yellow, red or brown or white spirits.

God's Purpose

We recently came across the question 'What is the purpose of God?' Well, do *you* know or know of anyone who could give a decisive answer to this or to the question, 'Is there a God?'

We say this because there are many people who do not believe that there is a God and there are many others who are very undecided. How can there be a God when he allows such terrible wars to take place and he does nothing to stop the misery that is in the world. We were talking to someone about religion and he said that he had no time for it or for God. He recounted the story of his sister, who had a little girl who, for the short time she was on the earth plane, suffered very badly through illness. Here he came out with the same old phrase of, surely if there was a God of love he would not want a child to suffer, so why didn't he stop it?

When we come into this world we are given a free will and that is why we are supposed to have a higher intelligence than the other animals although at times we wonder whether we have. Because of this free will we can and do just as we like, including things that are wrong and which can affect the well-being of others. We do not rest enough, we eat too much, we drink too much and we smoke too much, thus abusing our bodies to such an extent that we have to call on the doctor to help us but do we blame the doctor for our condition?

Once we knew a gentleman who professed to be a spiritualist, who was told by the doctors to ease up on his smoking which, of course, he did not do. When he had to go into hospital he moaned that with all the messages that he had received not one medium had told him that he would go to hospital. So when things go wrong or we become ill we blame mediums, we blame guides and, above all, we blame God or rather the non-existence of God. If the television, the sewing machine or car goes wrong, we get an expert in to check it and put it right but when our physical bodies are out of sorts, we cannot be bothered to see the doctor because we don't think as much of our bodies as we do the car. When we do go to see the doctor, we do not always take his advice and then we have the cheek to say that it is no good seeing him because he never does us any good. Is it the same with God?

We call upon God for help and then ignore his advice because we don't like the solution to the problem in the same way that we don't like the doctor's medicine. Let us remember that the nastiest medicine is often the sort that does us the most good and, even if some of God's remedies are not to our taste, they are all part of his purpose. Accepting that God is a personal being, let us realise that he is not interested in our physical bodies because he had no part in the making of them. These were made by our parents and that is why God cannot be blamed for the sickness of the child who we mentioned earlier or for any of our ailments. The part that God made, the part that makes us living beings, the only part he is interested in having back is alive and well or should be. The part we are speaking of is the spiritual one and the reason we are here on earth is to develop it so that it will grow in stature. When we begin to understand these things then we begin to know more about the purpose of God.

A lady we met some time ago was told that I was a medium and immediately she said, 'Oh I have seen that on television and I think it is a load of rubbish because I cannot believe in that stuff of there being a life after death.' When we asked her what she believed in, her reply astounded us, because she simply said, 'Nothing.' Surely people have to believe in something so that they can have a purpose in life even if that belief is only the hope of winning the pools. The very fact that God has given us a spiritual body means we have also been given a purpose.

In every walk of life from the most primitive to the highest civilised society we have rules, regulations and laws. We find them in governments, in town halls, tribal gatherings, sporting associations, throughout industry – they are there for the good of the community, acting as guidelines for those whom they affect. We read in the Bible of Moses giving the Ten Commandments to the Jews and later of Jesus bringing them up to date. In spiritualism we have The Seven Principles, which lay down guidance on how we should conduct our lives and, if we follow these principles, we are carrying out God's purpose, for they are not *a* way of life but *the* way of life.

God's Will

We hear a lot of talk of people putting up with circumstance because God ordained those circumstances or, to put it in simpler language, accepting things because it is God's will.

Occasionally, we used to visit an elderly aunt who was blind. When her husband was taken ill so that he had to go to hospital, she herself had to stay in an old people's home for the simple reason that she could not look after herself. She could have been a danger to her neighbours by turning on the gas, lighting a match and then not being able to find the stove again. Therefore she went into the home accepting everything in good grace saying 'It is one of those things so it is no good grumbling. After all, it is God's will.' This is a commendable attitude but we certainly do not believe that it is God's will that people should live in a world of darkness: people having to be led about shuffling and stumbling, especially when it is due to someone else's neglect or indifference.

Someone wrote a letter to a newspaper once in which she used the phrase, 'With faith in God we can turn away from our problems.' She was immediately given her reply by someone who said that the majority of Christians were too willing and too ready to foist their responsibilities on to God. This is very true and we must not look upon God as an insurance policy in the way people do when told that Jesus Christ died so that their sins would be washed away.

Some time ago, we took part in a forum of questions and answers and one of the questions was, 'With all the prayers for peace that are being sent out why has God not answered them and granted peace?' We feel that the questioner was thinking of the troubles in Northern Ireland but here again we have the foisting of responsibility on to God's shoulders while it appears that he has turned a deaf ear to our supplication.

However, shall we examine the predicament God may find himself in? During the last war, soldiers would attend church parade and the padré would ask God to bless their endeavours by granting them victory over the enemy. Amazingly, the padré of the opposing army was asking the same God an identical blessing. Talk about the brotherhood of man. Poor God, in such a predicament, so we would ask do we want peace at any price or peace at our price? In any decision we have to make are we willing to accept divine guidance or must it be what we want? If it must be the one we want then whose will is it?

God has given us stewardship not only of our physical and material matters but also of our spiritual beings with all that which is involved: our feelings, our emotions, our temperament, our thoughts. If we have developed these then we should have learned what to ask for and also how to ask for it. God is not responsible for starting wars so why should he be called upon to stop them and God is not the cause of anyone going blind or for suffering any physical afflication so why should he take the blame for it? The physical body was made by our parents and has nothing to do with God, so the only thing that he is interested in is the part of us given by him – the spiritual body or soul.

Unfortunately, as far as spiritual things are concerned, man is blind and refuses to be led, so he stumbles about in the dark making all sorts of mistakes. It is about time that we mixed the water with the dust and placed the mud on our eyes so that the scales will fall off them. Perhaps then we will be able to understand our steward-ship and comprehend the power that lies within us. The power that will enable us to understand ourselves. When we are able to do this, then we shall understand God's purpose rather than God's will.

Being spiritual, we are all part of that great power that most people call God, the source from which we came and to which we shall return. In recognising these facts shall we ask ourselves some questions? Could we or would we knowingly start a war? Would we knowingly be the cause of someone going blind or suffer some other physical affliction? We are sure the answer is no. So being part of that great power and if it is not our will to harm anyone, how can it be God's?

Eden and Paradise

As a start we would like to bring two phrases to you. The first, which we heard quite some time ago as part of a reading, was, 'It was perfect in paradise', and the second, a more recent one, 'You have to leave the Garden of Eden to start a life of your own'.

Now everything in that garden can be lovely, can be peaceful, can be tranquil and, in fact, it can be paradise. However, when we leave this paradise we find things are not so good or not so peaceful as we come up against the unpleasant things of this world. The words 'to lead a life of your own' denotes that we have been sheltered from the winds that blow but, when we decide to step out, then that shelter is not so noticeable.

We start with this introduction because some people think we should live in harmony with everyone, always being ready to turn the other cheek and we should see and show love at all times. Yet we say we must have these differences, these contrasts, the opposites or if you like the positive and the negative. Most people know that there are things in this world that do not mix. If they are mixed, then the result is an explosion. It is like walking into a room that has just been decorated and the colours hit you because they are harsh and do not merge together so that they are not pleasant to the vision.

We read that there was an intruder in the Garden of Eden who caused temptation. Like that intruder we have those who can be difficult, can be vindictive to such an extent they instill in us a feeling that is not good. We recall the words, 'Fear not him who harms the body but rather the one who harms the soul,' but we ourselves are the ones most likely to harm our souls by giving way to our feelings when we have been upset. This is a human failing, however. We are told that on one occasion Jesus lost his temper and gave vent to his feelings. In the knowledge of this we suppose we should dislike the wrong but be tolerant of the wrongdoer.

We have just mentioned the human failings and on this plane of thought we are dealing with the rougher and baser things of life. Someone we knew moved into a new house and when we visited we remarked how fine the soil was but they said that it was no good because the plants would not take root so they were going to mix some rough soil with that which was already there. Now when we are in paradise, Eden or the spirit world – call it what you will – perhaps we become too fine and therefore have to come to earth to mix with the rougher soil.

Earlier we mentioned colours and we would like to say something about how they can affect us. Each one of us has an aura encircling our body which is made up of various shades of colours and these denote the conditions of our body, physically, mentally and, most important, spiritually. Some people can see these auras but we feel that a lot more of us can sense them because we are drawn to some folk but are repelled by others. When we meet someone who repels us it could be that the colours or shades in their aura do not mix with ours and so immediately a barrier is built between us, whereas the colours of another person merge with ours and so there is an affinity between us. It is similar to certain plants growing next to each other in the garden where, because of their make up, they are poison to each other.

Colours are being used more and more in healing and even the experts, the specialists on earth, are discovering that certain colours have different effects on people. Maybe we are beginning to use the colours that are found in paradise.

We have something similar in circles where a group of people are sitting to develop their gifts with each sitter having something to offer. Although their gifts may differ each aura must merge with the others before they can become successful. Sometimes for the benefit of the circle, a sitter has to leave so that the circle can make further progress.

One young man used to sit in a circle but did not seem to get too much. However, he had some wonderful power and he used to ask some fascinating, some very deep, questions that created a lot of discussion. This is the way to find paradise so let us follow the young man's example and we are sure we shall find the peace of mind that is paradise.

3
Similarities

Knowledge, Wisdom and Understanding

Knowledge – that which we know
Wisdom – experience and knowledge with the power to judge rightly
Understanding – intelligence

Intelligence or intellect is insight but most important, experience, wisdom, knowledge are nothing without understanding.

When we first started work we met a man, in a responsible position, who knew his work inside out because he had the knowledge and the wisdom which years of experience had given him. However, his one big fault was that he could not impart his knowledge to others for he did not have the understanding of how to teach others. Since then we have met many people with the same problem. People who have authority, possibly through their wisdom and knowledge, but who are lacking in understanding even of those over whom they have authority, not realising that some have to be driven and others have to be led.

We were watching a religious programme on television in which the Salvation Army were taking part. Each member of the group spoke in turn of their daily work and how it had affected their religious beliefs. The Salvation Army representative, who was playing the organ, was not only company secretary with one of the largest organisations in the world but was also a magistrate. When asked how he viewed his position as a justice of the peace, he said he felt that he should put himself in the place of the person standing in front of him, try to understand him or her, understand his or her thoughts and in so doing try to help. You see this man, by his position and his work, had knowledge and wisdom but he still sought understanding.

There was a programme on radio about a healer who must be known throughout the world and who has a daughter, who by seeing the work of her father, must have knowledge and maybe wisdom of it. She must have seen some of the so-called miracles and yet she said she did not believe in life after death. We would ask where did she think her father's power came from to do his work? Did she think it was all due to his own efforts? She has knowledge of her father's work because she has seen the results but she is lacking in the deeper wisdom, the understanding.

We have this with a lot of people who have religious knowledge. They have education and wisdom which they can use to discuss their religious beliefs but when it comes to practising them they are lost. They do not know how to put theory into practice. They will argue that their beliefs are the best but anyone taking their actions as an example would not think so. We cannot understand why anyone argues about beliefs when we are all going to finish in the same place eventually.

This brings us to the disciples who were very fortunate because they lived with Jesus Christ and were able to observe his works, hear his words, listen to the parables but when he said, 'I go to prepare a place for you and wither I go ye know', they hadn't a clue what he was talking about. After all the knowledge they had been given, the wisdom imparted to them, they did not understand the meaning of any of it. It was the same with the woman who came to draw water from the well. Jesus promised he could give her living water which would so satisfy that she would never thirst again. How could this be when she had tasted this water before and she was always thirsty later? She was making the mistake we all make by looking at things in a material way rather than in a spiritual one. We must become as Samuel with Samuel's mind and his faith.

We must have some knowledge because we are sitting in a spiritualist church but do we have any wisdom or understanding? We probably know that there is life after death and through this it is possible to communicate with those who have 'died'. Then what? Do we understand what we can do with this knowledge? Someone asked what developing circles are for and how does one know if a medium is good? Circles are for gathering knowledge and for developing wisdom but we cannot become a good medium until we have the understanding of that wisdom. One further point: never think we know it all for the book of life is never-ending and self-praise is no recommendation.

Development and Achievement

Many towns and cities in this country, during our lifetime, have undergone great changes, with much demolition and development. Schemes have been put into operation to get rid of slums and also to ease the flow of traffic by getting rid of bottlenecks.

However, whilst all this work is going ahead there is quite an upheaval with large areas being flattened as if they had been hit by a bomb. In all this chaos have we thought of all the work and planning that must go into these schemes?

First, we have the surveyors along looking at the sites and noting the buildings that have to be demolished while at the same time we have experts taking samples of the soil so they can test it to see if it is suitable for the purpose they have in mind. While this is taking place, draughtsmen are at their boards, making various drawings and plans so that the best scheme can be chosen. When the idea is finally chosen and the go-ahead given, then an army of labourers move in to demolish the old buildings.

Then we have those who start the rebuilding, beginning with those who do the most important part of all – the digging and rebuilding of the foundations. Of course today they have all sorts of mechanical apparatus to help them. When the trenches have been dug, great loads of concrete are poured into them so that the foundations will be strong and firm.

From the foundations we can watch the buildings and roadways taking shape before the craftsmen – bricklayers, carpenters, glaziers and electricians – take over. The first two are involved with the actual building while the others are responsible for bringing light to it. The glaziers do it by bringing in natural light and the electricians by creating man-made light for when it gets dark. Of course, as all this work is being carried out, it can cause a lot of inconvenience and worry but what an achievement when it is finished.

We realise that you do not want to hear a lecture on civil engineering so we will move on to the spiritual aspect of what has gone before. The lives we are living here can be likened to those development areas because they could be a monotonous, humdrum type of life. Maybe we have been letting things slide and our property is in need of repair or perhaps the traffic is grinding to a standstill so that we are making no headway.

We may realise that things are not as we would like them but feel that the work is beyond our capabilities so we shall have to call in the experts. Therefore we turn to God, we look to the church, we may even ask our spirit friends to help but the only trouble is that we are not patient enough to give the experts time to start work. It could be that we don't like the look of their plans, not understanding that the planners have to use the land and materials that are available. The surveyors have to plot out the land so we have to be tested like the soil, to see what we are best suited for, because it is no use wanting to be a healer if we haven't the healing gift. It is no good wanting to be clairvoyant if we do not understand the signs and symbols. Only when we accept this can the right type of foundation be built and, more important, the right helpers that are needed to lay that foundation.

The bricklayers start to repair some of our tarnished brickwork and the carpenters put in new doorways and windowframes that will create new visions, new opportunities and new openings for us. Glaziers will fix new glass in the frames so that there will be no draughts or dust entering to make us feel cold or dirty. Through these windows come the inspiration, the new thoughts and ideas that are going to help us along the new roadways. The electricians bring us light and upliftment when things are getting dark and dreary so that the mists and fogs will be removed from our minds. Just a word about electricity for, we all know that if we overload the circuit, we will blow a fuse, so do not expect too much power to start with. On the other hand do not keep the blinds drawn once the windows are fitted because there is nothing like natural inspiration.

We must understand that we are part of a team and those experts consider themselves as part of the same team. They bring enlightenment and opportunities to us and it costs us nothing except that we trust them and pull in the same direction so that we can use those opportunities to progress. By saying that we mean that we should accept their guidance without question once we come to know them.

We have heard people say that when they have done some spiritual work they feel depleted but we cannot understand this. They must be physically ill or they are not in tune with their guides and helpers. If we are attuned properly, far from being depleted, we should feel uplifted.

Circumstances and Conduct

These thoughts come to you because of some words we read, the words being, 'Circumstances are beyond the control of man but his conduct is in his own power.' From time to time we find ourselves in circumstances which are not to our liking and although we have just opened by saying that circumstances are beyond the control of man, we must also say that man is not always blameless. Living in a material world, it is always easy to forget that we are spiritual so that when we see or plan something we want, then we chase it irrespective of other people or their feelings. Therefore we create circumstances through our own conduct and that conduct is sometimes so bad that we make other people's lives a misery.

Let us take the example of someone who is given authority at work. When people accept the authority they recognise that circumstances have changed but their mistake is in not understanding how, because they think that with the power granted to them they can dictate to others. They do not realise that with the power they now possess they should be helping others along their pathway. In the same way, we have people who experience some good fortune in a material way but again their conduct leaves much to be desired. Their attitude is eat, drink and be merry, never giving a thought to those around them who may be in need of help. Again let us turn to examples. The first is someone who bought a new piece of furniture and then looked around to see who they could give, we repeat, give the original piece to and we are pleased to say he immediately found someone. The second example concerns a person who, due to alterations carried out in his house, had to buy new carpets because the old ones did not fit. The old carpets were put in the loft where they gathered dust, dirt and damp so that they became unuseable. And this was a person who could afford to give them away. Our philosophy is that all wealth should be shared, whether it be spiritual, material or through guidance and knowledge.

So what about ourselves, our conduct, our attitude to life, especially when we wake up in the morning? Do we have a little moan and say we wish we did not have to go to work? Why don't we realise how lucky we are? If we paid a visit to a hospital, we would see people who cannot get out of bed let alone go to work. Speaking of hospitals, we have to say that many of the patients conduct themselves with more dignity than those who visit them. In fact, some of the so-called friends and loved ones cannot sacrifice one hour of their time to visit. This is one instance where we could say that wealth is not being used as it should be.

We heard of a man who needed hospital treatment but was not able to receive it because there were no beds available. Eventually he was admitted to a hospital controlled by a religious organisation but was then discharged because he was not of their order. Not much Christian conduct there. Surely the teachings of Jesus Christ taught more than that because by evicting the merchants from the temple he showed that the spiritual was more important than the material? Or did he? We remember seeing a play in which he was shown as an anarchist and rabble-rouser, which is a totally different image from the accepted one. However, no man could have done the things that Jesus did if he was a rabble-rouser. He must have had a code of conduct because of the way he acted during the events leading up to his death. That conduct so affected one of those who died with him that Jesus promised that they would both be together in paradise.

On to spiritual things, because if we wish to progress in a spiritual manner then we must have a code of conduct. In our opening paragraph are two words which we have not touched upon yet and those words are 'control' and 'power'. Whilst talking to you we are receiving a power and we trust that we are controlling and conducting it in the right way. As we sit in circles we are given this power and, as the circles are schools in which we learn about spiritual matters, we should also learn how to use this power. We must use this power to become sincere and to seek for the highest because in spiritual as well as material, like attracts like, and if we do not conduct that power in the right way, we may draw to ourselves those who are not very nice. So you see we have control of the circumstances. How we use them depends on our conduct.

Mediums, especially, should control the power and conduct themselves properly, always recognising that the guides are part of a team and if the mediums are not going to be sincere how can they expect their helpers to be any different?

Once we were advised by a medium that if we having difficulty in giving clairvoyance to someone we should make some excuse and move on to another person. This is not the attitude or conduct we should adopt because we feel that a circumstance like this is a challenge. Let us conduct ourselves in a way in which we can control the circumstance and face the challenge.

Sincerity and Honesty of Intention

As we travel to and from churches we have many experiences, hear many remarks and proposals. Some are quite helpful, others not so and some are downright disturbing. In fact, some of the people we speak to are very much alarmed by a number of things that are taking place in our churches. They are upset about people who profess to have certain beliefs but do not live up to them and therefore are not being sincere. Most people today, when finishing a letter, end with 'Yours sincerely' even to someone they have never met. Makes one think.

Sincerity is purity of heart, honesty of mind plus honesty of intention. When we look at these definitions we realise how much we fail by timid excuses, through broken promises, telling lies and letting others shoulder our responsibilities. We also fail when we blame others and the circumstances around us when things go wrong.

We know of a gentleman who, when asked by someone if they should do a certain thing, would give his advice but would also tell the inquirer that the final decision should be his or her own. By giving this last piece of advice, if things did go wrong then the only one to blame is the one who made the decision. This man was wise because the giving and receiving of clairvoyance should be governed by the same rule. We all have free will which enables us to make decisions and if clairvoyants tell people that they must or must not do something then they are taking away that free will. In fact they are controlling those people's lives.

Of course we have people who seek advice from clairvoyants so that any decision will be made for them but of course if something goes wrong then it is the medium who is blamed. This is an instance of others shouldering our burdens.

We recall an occasion when we gave a gentleman some advice or guidance but he said no to everything. After the service we passed him along the road, so we asked him to give some thought to what we had said. However, he replied, 'Not likely. You did not tell me what I wanted to hear.' We do not always get what we want but rather what we need and in a lot of instances this does us more good.

A young lady came to church and was told by the medium that her mind seemed to be in a turmoil but, if she continued to come to church, she would receive help from the gentleman who was sitting behind her. After the service the gentleman did have a word with her but was told she did not want or need any advice. So there you have it. Someone not being honest but who would probably go outside and tell the world that the church did not help her.

It behoves us all to be sincere in our spiritual endeavours, whether it be in giving or receiving because, remember, there is an art in receiving as well as giving. For those of us who are fortunate to be able to help others let us be honest in mind and honest in intention.

We always remember a man telling us how easily and naturally his sister could see spirit people and yet did nothing with her gift, she never told others about it or tried to help anyone by passing on her knowledge. Another young lady admitted to seeing wonderful pictures and visions but told no one about them because she was not a spiritualist, although her mother was a medium.

We do not care what we call ourselves, whether it be Hindu, Muslim, Christian, or even atheist. Let others know of your experiences. Be honest, be sincere to those loved ones who make it possible for us to experience these wonderful things because they work hard on our behalf and their only reward is the satisfaction of helping us.

However, when we receive these blessings we must use them in the right way, use them in the sense of purity of heart and not in what can we get out of them through praise and self-importance. The important part or person is that which or who comes from spirit for, without this contribution, we should be as nothing.

We listened to a medium giving clairvoyance. He was doing quite well, so well in fact that he became so cheeky and over-confident that he started giving bits from his own mind and what a mess he landed in. Another man could always take a service at his own church because he knew so much about the other members and he even had the cheek to admit it. We could all work like that. We could say something like, 'The sun is shining so things are going to brighten up' or 'We can see a field of corn so there is a harvest for you' and so we would claim that we had given a message. But what sort of message? We have not given any proof of where the message came from or life after death. To be sincere and honest we must give names, anniversaries and personal items or snippets that are only known to the recipient.

We have been privileged to be leader of a circle on a number of occasions and one of the things we have tried to instil into the sitters is that they must give proof as well as give an airy-fairy message. On a number of occasions we have had sitters drop out of the circle and we do not have to wonder why. It is the same with healing because the healer should be able to tell the patient what is wrong rather than the other way round.

You see not everyone who says they are mediums are necessarily so, not everyone who wears a white coat is a healer and not everyone who comes to a spiritualist church is spiritual. What we are saying is that many people go through the motions of being spiritual so long as they can stand up and bask in the limelight. They say we belong to this group or that association and have certificates for this, that or the other, but do these things make them spiritual or more sincere?

On one occasion we were asked why a young man who had been going to a healing group for some length of time showed no improvement and yet when an individual gave him healing he started to improve. Could it be that the group wanted to heal him so they could get some self-glory and the lone healer wanted to see him better? That is purity of heart, honesty of mind and honesty of intention.

Belief and Faith

The dictionary says belief is 'to have faith' and describes faith as having 'trust and belief', but it also says it is 'the assent of the mind to the truth of what someone else is saying', which means that what someone else says is 'the truth'. Because of, and in spite of this, we say that there is a difference between 'faith' and 'belief'.

We can read something in a book or magazine and say to ourselves 'that is feasible, it is something I could believe,' but would it give us faith in it? Again we are told there are pyramids in Egypt and a bridge across Sydney harbour and we believe these things because we have seen pictures of them but if we had not seen the pictures and had to rely on someone's word, would we have faith that they existed? If we had cancer and the doctor said that he could cure us, we may believe him but do we have the faith to know he would?

We are told there is life on other planets and maybe we accept these claims but do we really believe them or have faith to think they are true? All religions teach that there is life after death but how many people in this world have belief or faith in these teachings? Having been told there is a heaven, summerland or spirit world, would we have the faith to know that there is one?

A lady once said that she knew there was a spirit world but how many listening to her would accept her statement? However, this lady was convinced because one night whilst she was asleep, her mother came and took her on a tour of the other world so, because she had seen it, she knew it existed. Now we come to church so we must have heard of heaven or the spirit world but do we have enough faith to accept that one day we shall leave our loved ones to go to live there? Before you say yes, ask yourself this question, 'If it is so good in the next world, why do we fight to stay here?' Have we enough faith to know that when we go from this earth, we shall be able to come back and visit?

We are really Doubting Thomases because we are told that we have spiritual gifts and yet do not have the faith to use them. We are told we can heal by the laying on of hands or through thought power, but we are afraid to reach out. Our doubting minds say, 'If I don't succeed, they will think I am a failure', showing that we believe that we have these gifts but haven't the faith to use them. What about when we are told that we should be able to see, hear or even sense spiritual things? Most of us believe that this is possible but, when we do experience them, we put it down to our imagination. When we change this attitude and become positive by saying we have seen or heard then we are demonstrating faith, not only in our ability but also in the guides. Some people do not believe in anything and even ridicule others' beliefs and faiths. One family who professed not to believe in anything sent out the wish, when their mother was dying that the father should come to fetch her which makes one wonder where he was coming from and, more important, where was he going to take her. We suppose that when the lady passed, the family believed she was with her husband.

People say they have faith in a certain medium because that medium gives good evidence but what they should be saying is that they have faith in the guides because it is they who pass the evidence to the medium. At one service we spoke to a couple who would accept only one thing about someone who worked on the railways but could not accept names, dates or illnesses. After the service, the president of the church, himself a medium, said, 'Don't worry about them saying no. They can say it a thousand times but if your guides have shown it to you then you have seen it.' That is faith and it is the faith that all mediums should have in their guides. It is not sufficient to say 'we believe they are there', for we should have faith to know that the things that are being put into our minds are being put there by the guides.

A lady once approached us for advice but when we told her she should take a certain course she declined the advice and went in the opposite direction. In fact, she told me in no uncertain terms that she did not think much of me for suggesting such a solution. Now this lady was a pensioner and the way she wanted to go would have cost her money, which she could not afford, and we were convinced by the guides to persuade her to take a different pathway. We could have told the lady what she wanted to hear but that would not have shown much faith in the guides and this was proved some months later when the lady apologised and said that we had been right.

So let us cast out any doubts and go forward in the truth that faith in our guides can remove mountains.

Psychic and Spiritual

Recently we have heard of people using psychic gifts in the name of spiritualism. – Note, we said 'psychic'. In the dictionary, psychic is said to be 'appertaining to the occult' but there is also the word psychical which is 'of phenomena or conditions outside the physical law'. Anything outside the physical law is a mystery to most people and because of this their interpretation is inclined to be of a spiritual nature.

Now to the word 'occult', which is said to be mysterious, secretive, magical and involving the supernatural. Spirit is the animating or intelligent part of man, most times referred to as the soul and, as such, is not connected with the physical body. Oh dear, isn't that a contradiction? If the spirit is the animating part of man then it must have something to do with the physical body. The word 'spiritual' is of the spirit as opposed to the physical, of the soul and proceeding from God.

Most people would define spiritualism as the belief that the spirits of the 'dead' can communicate with the living through a medium. What an idea. It is like saying that you are a Roman Catholic because the priest forgives your sins or the only reason you go to the Church of England is to be given holy communion by the vicar. So we ask the question, is that what spiritualism really is? And we are sorry to say that this is the impression of a lot of people. Yes, even some of those associated with spiritualist churches. No wonder the psychic, the occult and spiritualism are all lumped together and people say that it is supernatural or supernormal. It is quite a natural way of life and there is nothing supernormal about it. It is only mysterious and magical because most people have no knowledge of spiritualism or of its true meaning, its true message, its aims and if they come to church it is because they want a message.

However, spiritualism is more than the giving and receiving of messages. It is about love, compassion and the way we conduct our lives here so that we are fitted and prepared for our existence hereafter. We have heard said, 'I am not going to listen to that medium because he dwells too much on the philosophy and does not give many messages.' The giving of messages has its place inasmuch that it proves that our 'lost' loved ones are still living and can come back to comfort us. In saying this, we must remember the most important thing is proving communication between the two worlds and not giving a message.

A young lady was being given a message about some jewellery that had been left to her when someone had passed away. She said it was the ring she was wearing which had belonged to her grandmother who had passed away ten years previously. The girl's mother had only given it to her the week before. The medium could have passed on to other things but he was not satisfied and asked about another piece of jewellery and the girl said there was another ring but her mother thought it was too valuable for her to have at the present time. The medium then asked about a necklace and the girl replied, 'That is quite right but I had forgotten it.' This type of message not only demonstrates life after death and communication between the two worlds but also squashes the theory of telepathy between the medium and the sitter because, in this instance, the sitter had forgotten the main item of evidence.

Everyone has some sort of gift but they do not always develop it. Some folks do but only to a certain point when they feel they have learned enough. These are the psychics and we are sorry to say that these people are concerned not so much with the spiritual as with the material. They are also becoming involved with spiritual churches so that they can ply their wares.

Even some mediums feel that when they have reached a certain point in their progression they have gone far enough and we feel that this is sad, in fact, it is tragic, because no one can progress far enough on this plane of thought. These people feel that they should not sit, that there is no need for them to sit in circles or discussion groups to learn about spiritual matters. We feel strongly that this attitude must change because we must have those who can teach others and, if we are going to stop learning in the third form, how are we going to teach those who wish to reach the sixth form?

As we travel around the various churches we have people who ask us how they can develop and in a lot of instances this is asked by youngsters. This upsets us somewhat because these people may have attended the church for quite a time but no one has bothered to speak to them and ask if they would like to join a circle. When we talk of developing we mean in a spiritual, and not in a psychic, sense. Sometimes we are able to listen to the notices being read out at the end of the service. We hear that the church holds two or even three clairvoyant services per week but there is no mention of a developing circle or discussion group. Once we heard that there would be bingo on one night in the week but there was no mention of a developing group. Now we know there should be social activities in the church but not at the expense of spiritual unfoldment. Our belief is that all churches should have the facilities for teaching the philosophy of spiritualism rather than concentrating on being able to give clairvoyance because this can be developed as we are learning about philosophy.

The first thing we should remember during our development is that we should have love and compassion in our endeavours. By saying this we mean that if we start to do healing we do so because we want to make someone better and not so that we will look clever and important. This applies to all gifts because we feel that if we are bringing someone comfort then we are healing them. We are giving them peace of mind.

We met a young man once who asked about developing his gifts and after a couple of weeks someone asked him why he wanted to develop and he said he enjoyed good health, had a good home, a good job and a marvellous wife to share it with so he thought it was time to give something back for what he had been given.

On the other side of the story is the lady we heard of who was receiving healing in her home, which meant that the healer had to visit her. After a time the healer thought she was not doing enough to help herself so he asked if she could visit the church for healing. She refused emphatically, so he told her that if she could visit the hairdresser's once a week then she could come to church occasionally. He gave her a month to make up her mind but, sad to say, the healing came to an end.

There is another lady, who we know personally, who was told by the hospital doctors that they had done all they could for her so she would have to go home and stay in bed. But this was the last thing this lady intended to do. She too received healing and one day said to the healer, 'That's right, let me hold your hand because I want to say a little prayer,' but she was not praying for herself but for two or three of her neighbours who were sick.

That is the attitude to be adopted because that is the way the spiritual helpers work. Not for them the self-glory but the spiritual progress so why shouldn't we follow their example? Let us see that only good spiritual mediums with a good spiritual message of philosophy serve our churches.

After all, we are fortunate to be able to worship as freely as we do because not so many years ago circumstances were so different. The pioneers of that time fought long and hard for spiritualism to

be recognised as a religion. Therefore let us see that their efforts
are not wasted.

Religions and Principles

We suppose, if we attended a spiritualist church regularly, we could call ourselves spiritualists but if you were asked to define a spiritualist would you be able to give a satisfactory answer? We ask this because we sat in the congregation of one church and afterwards we spoke to a lady who was attending a spiritualist church for the first time. We had the impression that it would also be the last, because she said that it was a load of rubbish.

What would happen if *we* went to a church of a different religion? Would we think it was a load of rubbish? What do we know of Buddhism, Taoism, Hinduism and, nearer home, the Hebrew religion or Christianity? If we examine them, we will find there are many things in these religions that are akin to spiritualism, so shall we do just that.

Buddha was heir to the throne of one of the Hindu tribes but he gave up his easy life with all its riches because of all the poverty and disease that he could see around him. Thereafter, he wandered about as a monk, caring for his fellow men, looking for an answer to the inequalities of the world. When understanding came, he realised the answer was in the law of karma – from good shall come good and from evil shall come evil. Because of his compassion for his fellow men, Buddha has been likened to Jesus Christ. Buddhists believe in something they call 'nirvana', which means complete attunement with the divine power. To achieve this the soul must experience several incarnations, each one spiritually higher than the previous one. Compare these few observations with the principles of spiritualism. Buddhists believe in the fatherhood of God through the attunement with the divine power, the brotherhood of man because of their compassion for their fellow men, the continuous existence of the soul because of the various incarnations and, because each incarnation has to be higher than the previous one, they believe in the eternal progress of every soul.

The followers of Taoism offer sacrifices, through mediums, to their ancestors. In this way, they hope that the spirits of their ancestors will possess the mediums. They believe that, if the mediums can rid their minds of all worldly and materialistic thoughts and at the same time quieten all physical and mental activities, it is possible to have intimate discussions with higher spiritual forces. Under these conditions they believe that mediums could have such spiritual powers as to render the physical body immune from injury and disease. At death, the spiritual body goes to the 'Island of Paradise' and that which is left is an illusion. Again we have spiritual principles involved: the communion of spirits, the ministry of angels, the continued existence of the soul and eternal progress open to every soul.

The Hebrew religion, in its early days, was probably based on folklore and there would be several gods. This was due to the fact that after an elder died, his relations saw him, sometimes in dreams or visions, so he would be looked upon as a god. Thus came the saying we read so much in the Old Testament: 'I saw God', when, in actual fact, they saw the spirit of their loved one. Eventually, through the patriarchs and especially Moses, the various gods were dismissed and only one god, Jehovah, was recognised. The Jews are still waiting for the Messiah to come so we are not sure whether they are convinced of life after death although they had enough psychic experiences to persuade them. How many times in the Old Testament do we read: 'God said to me' or 'God appeared to me'. What of the instances of transfigurations and manifestations? Most of the mediums responsible for these phenomena were as good if not better than those of today. These events prove that the phenomena of today are nothing new. Because of this evidence, written evidence believed by millions in the world of today, we have the fatherhood of God, the communion of spirits and the continued existence of the human soul.

It is said that Christianity was founded because of the birth of Jesus Christ but when we consider everything, maybe it was due to his death. From his teachings and through the example of the life he led, the ideals of Christianity were born. He was one of the finest mediums the world has ever known for, besides being a healer, he was clairvoyant, clairaudient as well as being a physical medium who participated in materialisations and transfigurations. Even when he picked his disciples he was inspired to choose those who had psychic gifts. He said of his gifts 'greater things than these shall ye do'. Up to the fifth century, mediums were allowed to work in the established church. Then the church threw them out because they were not following the dogmas and creeds that were laid down. The church admitted that what the mediums were doing was not wrong but it was against the church's beliefs.

The Christian church believes in the fatherhood of God and through the teachings of Jesus must believe in the brotherhood of man. It also believes that when anyone dies they go to a place called heaven and therefore they must acknowledge the continuous existence of the soul. We feel that the other principles do not apply because Christians believe in what is known as the 'vicarious atonement', which means that as Jesus was crucified, everyone's sins are automatically forgiven. As we see it, this is as good as saying that Jesus Christ is an insurance policy and that no one need be responsible for their actions. If they do not believe in personal responsibility then they cannot follow up with compensation and retribution for sins they have committed or for eternal progress open to every soul.

Now to spiritualism and to the principle of personal responsibility, which is totally different to vicarious atonement and, in our opinion, is the most important principle of all. It means that we are responsible for our words, our actions and above all our thoughts, not only on Sundays but on every day of the week.

We must have love and compassion and above all must be ready to appreciate other people's points of view, especially in relation to religions, because they are very much akin to spiritualism. We shall all finish up in the same place eventually.

Therefore, when we say we are spiritualists, let us remember the depth of what we are saying and, when we say it, let us make sure we are being spiritual.

Service and Reward

We call this 'service and reward' but it could so easily have been called 'work and wages'. However, although the phrases may seem to be similar, there is a difference. A reward is something that is granted to us and which we do not expect but a wage is something that is given and we do expect for work that we have done. In fact, a wage is a thing that is negotiated and even argued about before the work is started. Today we would say that the wage has assumed more importance than the work because the first thought is 'what is there in it for me' or 'what can I make out of it', irrespective of how the work is done.

Why, even when a guarantee is given, it is not always easy to get those concerned to honour it, so to have faults put right we have to pay out more money. Years ago, when people were more personally involved with their work, they had more pride in it but today, when it is mass produced at the touch of a button, they feel they have nothing to be proud of. Even when we draw our wages, we moan about that which has been stopped in the way of taxes and such things. We do not seem to realise that if we do not put something in the kitty, then we ought not expect to take anything out.

Let us now move away from work and wages to service and reward and, as we have said, when we perform a service we do not expect a reward so there is no need for negotiations or bargaining beforehand. That is how we feel it should be and therefore such thoughts as 'what is there in it for me' should not be entertained. When we speak of service and reward we are talking of the spiritual counterpart of work and wages and so we feel our first thought should be about the work we are going to do. After all those spirit workers who assist us do not look for reward; they come along quite voluntarily because they have a desire and a love to help their fellow creatures. However, we are sorry to say that there are those who sit in groups to learn about spiritual matters by developing their own spiritual talents who are not so interested in the service, work or even the helpers, as much as in what they themselves are going to get out of it.

When we make this statement we are not only talking about

money or material things but also those who would seek self-glory and praise. We can recall sitting in one developing circle to learn about spiritual matters where one of the sitters told the others that they should feel privileged to sit in the same group as she. We could not understand what she meant until one of the other sitters told us that she had spoken from the rostrum on a couple of occasions.

Now, we are not against anyone seeking the glory because eventually they are the ones who will lose and fall off the pedestal. We are not against anyone taking a fee, in fact, in some instances, we would recommend it but that which we speak against is when the reward, the glory or the fee becomes more important than the service. This is the material attitude of 'what is in it for me' creeping in, so let us remember that the guides and helpers do not ask for glory or a fee.

When we start out on our work of serving others we shall not be taxed except in the fact that we shall have to make sacrifices, mostly by giving up a lot of our time and possibly having to do things we would rather not do. Someone once asked us what the medium received for giving his services. First of all, we meet different people who have had various experiences and through these people and their experiences we gain knowledge. Then we have the privilege of being inspired by teachers, helpers and guides and, being so inspired, we receive wonderful power and upliftment, especially when we can bring a loved one from the spirit world to someone here on earth. The emotion is wonderful – something the words of this earth cannot describe.

However, it is not only mediums who are privileged to experience these things because we can all have love, help and guidance from the spirit world which we can share with others. We all cry out to God for help and then we blame him because we do not recognise the inspiration when it comes. If we try to develop our spiritual gifts, our spiritual senses will become so keen that, in tune with our spiritual friends, we will recognise and be able to act when we receive the inspiration.

So let us wake up to those spiritual senses but do not look upon it as a job of work because we may find it becomes a burden but rather see it as a service and we will find it becomes a pleasure. We will give you this guarantee that there will be no redundancies because we cannot get enough workers to fill the the vacant positions, so you can apply as soon as possible. Another guarantee is that the more you put into life the more you will get out through spiritual help, spiritual guidance and something that material wealth cannot buy – peace of mind.

Men and Machines

Today we live in a wonderful age, an age of machinery and invention. Throughout the ages man has made progress but we feel that during our lifetime on earth, this progress has quickened so much that he has advanced faster than ever before.

In the past someone invented something and another person, possibly in another part of the world, improved on it or maybe invented another object. Each object was independent of the others, different in shape and size, made of different materials and yet when assembled, became a wonderful piece of machinery. However, each one of these masterpieces has one common fault and that is that they go wrong. Like the new car, whose owner said that the dealer had had it in the showroom, more than he had in his garage and still it was not right, but of course this can happen to all these machines.

Now before these inventions are manufactured, plans and drawings are made and tests are carried out on each and every part, yet still things go wrong. Normally at the push of a button or the turn of switch these machines would work but because of some small fault, or even a speck of dust, they fail to do so. Although these things are guaranteed they are not made to last for ever and they are not expected to do so because we have what is known as depreciation. This means we get wear and tear, which makes the various parts thin so that they rattle and, when this happens, we have to get new parts fitted so that the machine will run smoothly again.

Now we can hear you saying, 'What has this to do with our lives?' Well, when we come into this earth if everything has gone right up to and including our birth, we are considered masterpieces but let us face the truth and admit that we do not always appreciate what wonderful machines our bodies are. However, things are not always straightforward and so we get a similar situation as that when a piece of machinery goes wrong. It is then that the specialists start investigating. This can be annoying but, looking on the bright side, let us remember these investigations may help others later. We knew a lady who was very ill with cancer whose son told the doctors at the hospital not to experiment but to let her die gracefully.

But his mother said, 'If by experimenting they can help someone else later then let them do it.'

As we have said, our bodies are such wonderful machines that it only wants one small part not to function properly for the whole body to be thrown out of gear. As with depreciation in manufactured goods, so with our bodies, because as we get older our reflexes become slower so that we don't move or do things as easily as we used to and our joints start to stiffen. Of course, today doctors are beginning to fit 'spare parts' to bodies and although they may not be as good as the originals, they do help the body to function. They may make living a little easier for the recipients but we do not think they add any extra time to their span of life. Let us remember that anything made by man will deteriorate, like the machines, so with our material bodies because they were made by man.

There is one part of us, however, that can never break down, never grow old or die and that is the part given to us by God. Call it the engine, the motor, the soul or the spirit, it is the part that drives us along and without it our material bodies would not function. No outside influence can hurt it – we are the only ones that can do that by not facing up to our responsibilities.

In our spirit bodies we have every emotion we can think of, love, hate, pride, shame, joy, sadness, surprise, disappointment and all the others, both positive and negative. We have to face up to all sorts of problems and decisions that affect our spiritual lives and how we face up to them is the thing that matters.

We teach ourselves how to use the machines that our fellow men make and we can manipulate our physical bodies in their material context, so what about our spiritual parts? Perhaps we do not think they are important enough. Perhaps we think of ourselves as a small part in a large machine we call the world but let us remember how important the small parts are. If we are only a washer or a bolt, maybe we are the part that will stop the machine from rattling.

Apprentices and Apprenticeships

An apprentice is someone who is learning a trade or profession. Usually we associate apprentices with the young but why this should be we do not know because apprenticeships are periods of learning and we are learning throughout our lives.

We used to know a man who was a craftsman in the building trade and his business took him into factories where he worked with all types of materials such as steel, lead, copper, brass etc, on boilers, plumbing and similar work. Now here was a man who you would have said had served his apprenticeship. However, when plastics first started to be used he took a course because he said it was something new which he did not know much about and he liked to keep up with progress.

Many large businesses run apprentice schemes with a special department called a training school where the young apprentices are taught the groundwork of their trade and this part of their training is the most important, because it is the foundation. We have heard people say that these schemes are a waste of time because the apprentices learn nothing and we would accept that an odd one or two do not take their training seriously but let us ask the question, 'Where do the craftsmen come from if the trainees learn nothing?' Apart from apprentices, businesses send managers, foremen and craftsmen on refresher courses so that they can keep up with new developments.

We suppose you are wondering what all this has to do with spirituality. As we talk to people about spiritualism a remark we often hear is, 'I suppose you were born with these gifts', and we reply that everyone is born with them, or at least one gift. Some folks do realise that they have a gift and try to develop it whilst others let it lie dormant. It is similar to going to school where the subjects we are interested in we find easy to learn but those in which we have no interest we find very difficult to absorb and so we are not very good at these subjects.

Many people tell us that they have learned more since leaving school than they ever did while at school and this is quite probably true. However, would they have learned anything if they had not been to school? Would they have been able to form words if they had not learned the alphabet? Would they have been able to keep accounts if they had not been taught how to add and subtract?

We tell you these things to show that man has been taught and tutored almost from the day he was born and has made enormous progress but only in a material way. So much progress that he can walk on the moon and in space but ask him where he came from or, more important, where is he going to and he could not give a satisfactory answer. We read in the Bible that Jesus said, 'In a little while I shall leave you and whither I go ye know', but the disciples did not know. Now they were very fortunate in that they lived and walked the earth with possibly the greatest medium known and yet when he was going to leave them, after all they had been taught, they knew nothing.

Almost two thousand years later, we still know very little so isn't it about time we learned our ABC to enable us to begin our apprenticeship? We hear phrases, as far as spiritual matters are concerned, like, 'Oh, I couldn't do anything' and of course it is true if we are not even going to try. Let us get into developing circles and begin to use our gifts because one of the weaknesses of spiritualism is not only the lack of circles but the right sort of circles. Let us remember that the circle is not only for giving and receiving messages but also for the teaching of spiritual matters, including spirituality.

There is no need for a large or grand building in which to hold a circle for, after all, the training centre in the factories only takes up a small area of the total space. Therefore our own homes could be used. We badly need the right sort of circles with the sort of sitters who are sincere and who will attend regularly and promptly. Let us make the rule that each sitter in turn opens and closes so that we shall find out whether they can do anything. We remember one circle where we applied these rules and at the second sitting only half the original sitters turned up, so we knew who the sincere ones were. After perhaps six or seven weeks everyone in the circle will have broken the ice by saying a few words of prayer and then will feel more comfortable about progressing further.

When we have progressed sufficiently to speak in public do not think that we have finished our apprenticeship because we must remember that we are only leaving the training school to go into the workshop. It is a great pity when mediums speak in public they think there is no need to sit in a circle, so let us think about the man who took a course in plastics and follow his example.

Jesus Christ is said to have spoken in the temple at the age of twelve but we hear no more of him until he was thirty. We would like to think he was in the training school during this time. From time to time, he also withdrew from the crowds and this poses the question – was he sitting quietly with friends taking a refresher course?

The fact that you are reading these words shows that you have some sort of interest but what sort and how much? A lady once came to church and asked who was speaking. On being told, she said, 'I am not stopping. I have been in the movement thirty years and don't wish to listen to beginners.' What the lady meant was that she had been receiving messages for thirty years but if she had been asked to say a closing prayer she would not have been able to do so.

Who are we going to be like, the lady with thirty years' 'experience' or the man who took a refresher course?

4
Sowing and Reaping

Seasons

We have all heard the saying: 'You will not be able to tell one season from another except by the falling of the leaves.' Sometimes the weather we experience makes us wonder what season it is because we can have a brighter and warmer Christmas Day than an August Bank Holiday.

Let us examine this subject of seasons, starting with the springtime of the year, taking in the months of March, April and May. The season of a new beginning and a new birth, of cleanliness and a tidying-up. When you think of the months of the season you can appreciate where the cleanliness comes in with the March winds blowing away the dust and dirt followed by the April showers to wash it all away. This is the season when the world of nature becomes alive, or rather when we see evidence of life, because nature never dies. Seeds and bulbs which have been lying in the dark soil start pushing their way towards the light and warmth so that we can see green shoots appearing. The animal world ends its hibernation and we hear again the sounds of the birds who have returned from their migration in warmer climates. We also notice the hours of daylight getting longer and the days themselves becoming brighter.

Now on to summer when the promise of spring should materialise: the time when everything should blossom to its fullest, when the seeds, bulbs and green shoots become flowers, plants or shrubs and when we see the trees in all their glory. Judgement can then be passed whether the sojourn of the seeds in the soil has been beneficial. This is the time when we expect plenty of sunshine but let us remember that too much sunshine is not always good for us because it can bring headaches, stomach upsets and, very likely, thunderstorms. Too much sun without rain can mean that the soil is going to become dry and parched and will certainly not do the plants any good.

The next season is autumn when we notice the process of spring going into reverse. The days get shorter, the weather becomes more cold with the possibility of early fogs and frosts. The leaves on the trees begin to change colour, becoming red, brown, gold and start to drop to the ground and at the same time the birds leave for warmer climates whilst the animals take in a stock of food before hibernation. Sometimes we have what is known as an Indian summer when the sunshine stays with us just a little longer than usual, thus making the winter shorter.

Whichever way it is, we still have the season of winter to follow with its fogs, frost and snow. This is the season of sleep and darkness. Please note we said sleep because the world of nature does not die although the trees look as if they are dead. When spring comes round again we shall see them come to life.

Back now to spring but this time in a spiritual sense and again it heralds a new beginning, new thoughts, a tidying-up and a shaking-off of the dust. We are travelling along this earth plane feeling miserable, dissatisfied and maybe a little sorry for ourselves when the realisation comes to us that we are too self-centred and that we are not put on this earth for our own selfish ends. This awareness and awakening is similar to the birds and animals knowing when it is spring. We begin to realise that we are spiritual beings as well as physical and so the March winds blow away the dust and cobwebs whilst the April showers wash away the dirt that has been holding us back.

With the understanding that we are spiritual beings we also find that we have spiritual gifts that can be used not only for our own benefit but also as guidance for others and, as we use them, they begin to push their way through the dark soil like the green shoots of nature.

The spirit friends and guides come closer because we are learning how to use our gifts. So the outlook becomes lighter and brighter. This is the most important season because as we are nursed and educated in a material sense so we must learn lessons spiritually. This is the the season of foundation.

So spiritually, the summer is the season that shows our progression and from it others can tell what our spring was like: if the foundation was firm, if the soil was good and if the gardener had done his work well. The season when we begin to bloom and show ourselves in all our glory, but let us heed the warning that we must not bask in too much sunshine. Do not boast about what I can do so that we give others the impression that it is all *my* own work. If we do we may find the earth becomes dry and the water (spiritual power) is not reaching the roots and, in consequence, the flowers, the plants (our spiritual gifts) begin to fade.

Now on to the autumn, which we call the mellow season, the season of maturity and experience when through those experiences we have had in our earlier seasons we should be able to give advice and assistance to those who are just pushing their way through the springtime of life.

By so doing, we can lay in our winter supplies and may even enjoy an Indian summer. As the leaves and the seeds begin to fall, let us see that they fall upon fertile ground so that the fruit that will grow in the next spring can be of benefit to others. The winter season can be one of severe frosts and thick fogs that make it long and drear but if we have used our previous seasons well it could be more to our liking. It depends on how we have used the sun, the rain and the soil. This is one winter that we all have to face in which we all have to leave the earth plane to go through the mists and fogs but, unlike the material winters, we will not be able to book a cruise so that we can seek the sun.

In spite of this, there should be no fears, no anxiety and definitely no mourning because, when we emerge from the mists, we shall experience a spring and summer the like of which we have never known before.

Harvest Thanksgiving

As we look at the harvest we realise we have before us the fruits of much labour. We plough the fields and scatter the good seed on the land but that is not the end of it because the land is fed and watered by God's almighty hand through the snow, the gentle rain and the warmth of the sun.

Preparing the land is not as easy as it sounds because the soil must be of the right texture and mixture to suit the seeds that are to be planted. We were speaking to someone who had just moved to a new house and we asked how he was managing with the garden. When he said he had dug it over, we suggested it was now ready for planting. 'Oh no, the soil is much too heavy. It is nearly all clay and we shall have to dig it again so that we can break it up.' His problem was the exact opposite to someone else we knew whose soil was so fine that the plants would not stand up in it. What they both needed was a lorry-load of soil to mix with that which they already had to give it the right mixture for the plants to take root.

When we have attended to the soil, then we plant the seeds and then we must have patience while nature does its work. We must let the snow do its work of cleansing the ground, we must tolerate the frost which cleans the air. We must also be patient whilst the rain falls to give nourishment, followed by the sun which swells the grain. Of course, we would like all these things to come at the right time and in the right quantities. It is when we see the green shoots pushing their way through the earth that we must become aware because we must tend and nurture them against any extremities that could harm them.

As we come into this world as babies we are like the seeds being placed into their various plots and those first tender years are the most important. The harvest that will follow those early years will show what type of soil we are growing in and also whether we have been cared for and nurtured in the proper way.

Unfortunately, we could be born into soil that teaches us to be selfish, cruel, greedy and thoughtless so that we are the seeds that fall by the wayside on stony ground, with the result that we wither away or at most produce a poor harvest. Perhaps we push through the soil and begin to grow but find the going so tough that, as the pressures build up, we just stop trying. We could even be drawn away from the good soil because we think the grass is greener on the other side.

Mentioning greener grass reminds us of an article we read about a man who loaned out a field to a neighbour for cattle grazing, except that at one time of the year the cattle were not allowed in part of the field. This part was fed with animal manure but the other part was fed with chemicals. The area that was fed with chemicals grew more quickly than the other half. The proof of the pudding was in the eating because, when the cattle were brought in, they made straight for the area that had been fed with natural manure. Although the grass in the other half grew more quickly, there must have been something missing and the lesson must be: we only get back that which we put in.

Again we could be tired of the weather, saying we cannot stand the snow and frost, the sun makes us listless and when the rain comes, instead of being refreshed, we feel as if we are being drowned. Why don't we realise that we have to experience these seasons of upliftment and disappointment so that we can achieve a good harvest? A little effort is needed, so instead of taking the easy way out by spraying some sort of chemical over the soil let us feed it properly. It is so easy to let things go to pot but by doing so we are allowing the tares and weeds to take over. Remember that weeds are the easiest things to grow, so why not try to grow something worthwhile? Surely if we can grow weeds we should be able to grow other things?

When we plant seeds they not only grow but they also multiply so that one seed becomes an ear of corn and, when flowers die, they leave behind pods that are full of seeds. When we lift the bulbs out of the ground, we find they also have increased in number. Why can't we be the same? We sing, 'Take my life that in thy oceans flow our lives may be richer and fuller.'

On entering this world we bring with us the spiritual seed given to us by God, so why don't we make our soil rich and textured so that the seed may grow and multiply? We could also find time to help others with their soil. Our last thought is – may God grant us a good harvest with enough seeds to spare for use in our future harvests.

Harvest Lessons

It always gives us pleasure when we are able to take part in a Harvest Festival service, especially when we look back through the year and and appreciate that people were wondering whether there would be an harvest because of the drought. Things were so bad that people were praying for rain.

A gentleman, listening to all this talk of praying for rain asked why there had been no prayers for life that was being destroyed and killed, meaning vegetation and animals that were being destroyed by man. The thought then struck us that prayers had rarely been said for those who experienced these drought conditions for six months every year.

Eventually the rains came and the water began to roll down the hills and mountains into the reservoirs. Mountains and reservoirs take our thoughts to a television programme about a European country in which there were mountains. It opened by showing water cascading down the mountain, turning into a river as it progressed and the commentator, who was swimming in it, saying that, although it was cold, it was refreshing and invigorating.

The programme showed how the water brought down earth and stones from higher up and how these got caught up on the banks, or sometimes became attached to something in the centre where they formed into small islands. Besides stones the water also brought down seeds, which had dropped from the trees and bushes higher up, and these seeds lodged on the banks or islands where, after a season, they took root. Eventually, they became plants, bushes or even trees. Of course, all this took time but nature, being what it is, was gradually able to beautify the landscape.

Now, although man could see all this beauty, he did not appreciate it but what he did recognise was the power that was coming from the mountain top and if he could only harness it he would be able to use it for his own benefit. Because of these thoughts they brought in the earth removers, concrete mixers etc so that they could build up the banks to make the water flow where they wanted it to. From this beginning, roadways, houses, shops and businesses were built.

This not only spoilt the landscape but also prevented the seeds from taking root. Each one of us is like the seeds that come from the mountain top: we all start out as equal because we all come from the same nursery and have been cared for by the same gardeners. We are swept down the rivers of life, bringing with us a freshness, a spiritual freshness, because the place we start from is a spiritual nursery where all the seeds are good. We have always maintained that in the first few years of our earthly lives we are closer to the spiritual world than at any time until we return there. Therefore, as we start from the top of the mountain with this freshness, we also bring with us an innocence and these qualities bring pleasure and upliftment to others.

On our journey we are caught upon the banks and small islands so that whilst resting there we can look around, learn lessons and take patterns from those who have taken root. Unfortunately, the patterns are not always good and so by copying them we begin to lose our innocence and freshness. We start mixing the concrete, the good soil begins to vanish and we become selfish in a way that we only think of ourselves. If only we could keep our natural way of life instead of becoming tainted with materialism, this world would be a better place – in fact, it could be a Garden of Eden.

As we have to suffer all types of weather in a natural sense we suppose we have to have these experiences in our progression while we are here but, despite them, we should be able to make the best use of our soil. We should not build concrete barriers where nothing will grow but rather show love and compassion, thereby helping others to plant their seeds and tend their gardens.

There can be no promise of a material harvest but we will be growing in good spiritual soil and if we do not have the quantity, we shall certainly have the quality. It is not only this year's harvest that matters but it is those that follow, so if we can plant good seeds this year then the ensuing ones have a chance of being good.

It is our attitude of mind that matters, so if we are selfish, greedy or always on the lookout to help ourselves and do not mind who we trample over, then our harvest has to be poor.

We cannot have a harvest of love if we sow seeds of selfishness. The material harvest is important in the material world but much more important is the harvest of the soul, so remember the seeds we grow here will help us in the hereafter.

Someone said, 'We come into the world with nothing, we go out with nothing and what we get in between we take off someone else.' Let us pray that what we take are spiritual lessons given to us from the example of others and, because we have been guided,

let us make sure that we leave behind some good seeds that can
be planted in other people's gardens.

Roots and Fruits

Trees are known by their fruits and not by their roots. Although this may be a true saying, do not dismiss the roots because without them there would be no fruits. As we look round the gardens, parks and fields seeing not only the fruits but the flowers, bushes and trees, we remark how beautiful they are, not realising the amount of work and energy that has come from the roots to make them so. The ground has to be of the right texture for the roots to become established and to grow because some soil may be too light, whilst other soil may be too heavy.

After all this effort, there are times when the blooms and the fruits are very poor and the harvest is disappointing. The weather plays an important part in the growth of the fruits and if we get too much or not enough rain or sunshine then the crop can be affected. Sometimes we suffer from frosts and the fruits will die due to the adverse conditions but, providing the roots are not affected, then new fruit will grow at the next harvest. It is the same when we pick the fruit because by doing so we are not doing any damage to the roots.

There was one year when we had no rain for months and everything became dry and parched which, in turn, caused fires that burned fields and forests. People were saying that the vegetation would never recover but, when the rain began to fall, so the green shoots began to push through the soil. The part that could be seen was dead but that which was hidden was still growing, which meant that the roots were still flourishing.

When we go to church we hear mediums expounding their philosophy or demonstrating their gifts sometimes we pass the remark of how good they are but do we realise how much hard work has gone into their efforts to make them good? We forget they have chosen the soil, tended it, nurtured it and have made sacrifices so that the part that no one sees is strong, so that the roots will continue to draw up the water to feed the fruits.

If we want to progress spiritually, we join a circle but we must be prepared to work hard, to make sacrifices and face the fact that to achieve anything is not going to be easy. It is going to take time for the fruits to grow but the more we persevere, the more abundant they will become, so please do not expect to be an overnight success. Let us realise there is a season for sowing, a season for growing and another for reaping. As the seeds need time to develop and grow, let us have patience for the right season before we step out. Maybe there will have to be some severe pruning before we can do so. Again it could be that our soil is not of the right texture and needs to be treated so that some of the materialistic ideas may be changed and our thoughts become more spiritual. Remember TLC cannot be bought and as some of you may be wondering what TLC is, we will tell you a story:

Some years ago a lady bought a magnolia plant and, reading the instruction for planting, she noticed that it should be treated with TLC and so both she and a friend tried to buy some. The lady managing the shop had never heard of it but said she was expecting a phone call from someone who would probably know what it was but, when the call came, it drew a blank. Then someone else read the instructions and said that TLC meant 'tender loving care'. Now we all know what it is, we have no excuse for not using it. Like all the other spiritual seeds, it was given us when we came to the earth plane and as such it is beyond price.

Some people come to church who call themselves spiritualists although they may not be spiritual, others come and say they do not want labels put on them because there are spiritualists and spiritualists. We knew a man who demonstrated in spiritual churches who called himself a clairvoyant, not a spiritualist. It does not matter what we call ourselves so long as we care for our roots so that people can admire our fruits.

5
Festivals

Choice – An Easter Message

We would like to bring some words to you that were handed to me:

> You can choose a ready guide in some celestial voice,
> If you choose not to decide you still have made a choice,
> You can choose from phantom fears or kindness that can kill,
> I will choose a path that's clear – I will choose free will.

These words were given to us by a friend whose work involved mixing with young people. Whilst she was discussing something with three or four of them, one young man sat with pencil and paper in his hand scribbling away. When the discussion had finished, he handed the pad to our friend with the above words written on it and underneath was the signature, 'Mark'. The line that impressed us most was, 'If you choose not to decide, you still have made a choice.'

In the Christian calendar, Easter is one of the most important festivals with Easter Sunday being most significant. But Easter is not about one day or even three days because the events that led up to it took place over a period of several weeks. In fact, there were three Sundays involved – Passion Sunday, Palm Sunday and Easter Sunday. The most important one was Passion Sunday because that is when the choice was made to go to Jerusalem, bringing with it the phantom fears as to whether the result would be satisfactory. It also brought thoughts of kindness that can kill, which to us means that through the love shown, the destiny could be forgotten and things could carry on as before. However, if this way had been chosen, there would have been no Palm Sunday, no Good Friday, no Easter Sunday or any of the events inbetween.

As we trace our steps along our earthly pathways we all experience the happenings of Easter because there comes a time when we have to make a choice and very often it is something we would rather not do. Here we have the phantom fears, but, in spite of them, we feel we are being guided although we may not recognise it. The guidance is the celestial voice that impinges on our thoughts whether they be phantom fears or kindness. Of course, when our

Passion Sunday arrives we can choose not to decide and thus take the easy way out but let us remember in so doing we are not making progress. Maybe we think we are safe if we follow the crowd, making no decisions and accept all that follows with no experience of Easter, no hills or valleys, no disappointments or upliftments along our pathways.

Let us make the decision and partake of the experience and thus sample the upliftment of Palm Sunday in the knowledge that we have done something about the problem. Of course, afterwards we shall have to face the testing time and trial, experience the waiting for the judgement but we are sure the verdict will be, 'We find no fault with this person.' In taking the positive attitude we shall have to taste the wormwood and gall of Good Friday but remember that if we experience the carrying of the cross then we must also taste the spiritual wine of Easter Sunday.

We picked up a book and turned to the fly leaf to see what the book was about and we saw the words, 'This is the story of a man whose life had an influence on many people who didn't even know him,' but it was not the story of Jesus Christ, although the Easter story has had its influence on thousands. We will not have much fame or influence throughout the world but we each have our own small worlds and we can show an example to others that may have an effect on them.

This is the age of reason and spiritualism presents a rational teaching which does not rely on blind faith for salvation but one which is based on fact concerning the future life of all men. People today will not accept life after death unless it can be proved conclusively to them. The basis of spiritualism is in demonstrating survival and its philosophy is eternal progress open to every soul. This progress means accepting Passion, Palm and Easter Sundays but, most importantly, Good Friday.

We feel that this is the important message of Easter and may God bless a young man named Mark for starting it off through his thoughts.

Mansions

'In my father's house are many mansions, I go to prepare a place for you.' We upon this earth plane look on a mansion as a large building with many rooms but it need not so be because our homes *can* be mansions. Note we said homes and not houses.

When we move into a new house we then start to make it into a home and this means a lot of hard work with thoughtful planning. There is decorating to be done and windows have to be measured so that curtains can be hung. There are carpets to be laid and furniture must be placed in the proper positions. All these things have to blend one with another so that when people look at them they are not shocked and put off by the clash of patterns and colours. Home is somewhere that is comfortable, not so much a luxury, a place where folks can feel at ease and where they know they can relax. Where they have the assurance that they can come again and know they are welcome.

That is how churches should be, a place that people find comfortable and wherein they feel at ease. A place where they know what is happening. The trouble with all churches and religions today is that those who attend, especially the younger ones, do not always understand the dogma and ritual, all the chanting and ceremonies that take place. They do not understand why everyone is so solemn and dull because they reckon that if religion is all it is cracked up to be then everyone should be dancing and singing with plenty of smiling faces about.

The Salvation Army is to be admired because most of their services seem to be so lively that we doubt whether anyone ever goes to sleep at one of them. There was a young boy of about ten or eleven years of age who went missing on several Sunday evenings and when this suddenly dawned on his mother and she said, 'Alan where have you been disappearing to?' the boy replied, 'I have been going to the Salvation Army, Mom, and it is great.' If only some youngsters would come to spiritualist churches, then go home and tell their parents that 'it is great'.

Now we suggest that if you have a stranger in your midst you go out of your way to make him or her welcome and make sure he or she knows what is going on. We have been approached on several occasions with the question, 'What is it all about?' and, unfortunately, it has been mostly young people who have asked. There was one instance that involved an older man who seemed rather awkward because he did not seem to know what we were talking about when we were giving him a message. We spoke to him after the service and he said, 'I am frightened of spiritualism and I am frightened of you.' We assured him that he had nothing to fear from me as I had been fed that day so was not going to eat him. After putting him at ease we had an interesting conversation during which we hoped we helped him by giving him some food for thought.

A medium once told us that he had accepted an invitation to take some private readings at someone's house but he would not go there again because the atmosphere was so stiff and starchy. He had even been asked to change his shoes before entering the room where the readings were to be held. We give these illustrations for two reasons. The first one is that if a medium is to work properly he or she must feel comfortable because if he or she is upset or worried in any way, those who work with him or her as a team, the guides and helpers, may not be able to get close enough to inspire him or her. Secondly, the congregation should also feel comfortable and here the medium must play his or her part. If the medium is going to be boring and long-winded, then those listening will start fidgeting, coughing and rustling the sweet wrappings.

Jesus said, 'In my father's house are many mansions' but we say there there are many mansions on earth and each of us possesses one. The physical body which we can see was made by man but the one inside it which we cannot see was given by God. This is the activating part of us and without it the physical would not function, in fact it would be dead. The unseen body is known as the spirit or soul.

So God has given us something to care for, something valuable, something precious and it is our responsibility to take care of it. Let us remember we have spirit friends who come along to help, not only us but themselves, so that they can progress. To them it is like coming to church so let us keep the church in good condition with a good atmosphere.

Jesus also said, 'Fear not him that harms the body [the physical], but rather he who can harm the soul [the spiritual].' The most likely ones to do that are ourselves.

I Go To Prepare a Place For You

There is a belief, in fact there has been a belief for the past two thousand years, that Jesus Christ was crucified to give us everlasting life and that he died so that any sins or wrongs we commit will be redeemed because he died on that cross.

We remember seeing an advert in the local newspaper that took up this theme and it started with the words 'You only live once' and ended with the statement that Jesus was the only hope. In between, the advert told us that you cannot transplant life, which to us is a contradiction. Transplanting in the sense they were talking about means renewing something that is dead but how do you renew something that is living? We agree with them on one point and that is that Jesus is the only hope but not in the same way as they mean. They believe that Jesus died to 'save' us but we have a different viewpoint.

When Jesus spoke the words 'I go to prepare a place for you and whither I go ye know and the way ye know', we feel people jumped to the conclusion that he was sacrificing himself for them. In fact, he was telling them that life was everlasting and so we agree that you only live once but it is a continuous existence. He had been trying to teach people how to reach those mansions by the life he had led here on earth but they did not understand. That is why he was astounded when Thomas said, 'Lord we do not know where you are going so how do we know the way?' We wonder how many more Doubting Thomases there have been since those words were spoken.

Do we know the way? Some of us do not know what we want in a material sense so there must be some confusion when we come to spiritual things. We do not realise the power that is within us and being ignorant of it means that it is lying dormant. But what is more important is that we do not know what can be achieved through that power, which to us is the bigger tragedy.

Of course when we have progressed a little, we can still stumble like the medium who had been doing public work for some years until one day, while sitting in a circle, she went over to heal someone. Her own guide told her to sit down because her gifts did not include healing. Mentioning this reminds us of another medium who said that as she had been demonstrating for forty years she should know how to give clairvoyance. We accept what the lady said but we can all make mistakes. We say no matter how long we have been studying we shall never know it all because we will never finish reading the book of life. How can we, when life is everlasting? There is always something new to be discovered and as we have professors and doctors here on the earth plane so there are experts and specialists in the spirit world who are forever guiding us through inspiration and new thoughts.

The trouble is that man calls out for help and when it arrives he does not recognise it because his spiritual senses are not keen enough to pick up the signals that are being sent out. Even when he does pick them up he will not always accept them because they do not fit in with his plans and it could mean making sacrifices.

We travel along our spiritual pathways until something new that glitters like gold attracts us and we forget where we are heading. We gain a little elementary knowledge that tells us that life is immortal and perhaps, this is more important to a lot of people, that it is possible to communicate with those who have gone from here to a fuller life. However, what about the deeper spiritual message and truths? When we come into this world we bring with us spiritual attributes in the same way as we have sight, hearing, speech and so on and Jesus by his example taught us how to use them so why aren't we doing so?

Let us follow his example and by doing so we shall start to build those mansions he spoke about and let us remember that the more willing we are to help others, the better the materials we shall be using. Let us heed that we not only belong to this world but also to the one which follows and the door between is always ajar. Do not wait until we are called but let us knock, push, enter and partake of the spiritual food and wine that is waiting for us.

Whitsun

Recently we have read two phrases, the first one being 'The light of the world has gone out' and the second, 'The lord has sent an angel', that could have some meaning for the Sunday we call Whitsun or Whitsunday. The word is derived from White Sunday, when those who are baptised wear white to church.

This wearing of the white always took place seven weeks after the Passover and the festival was known as the Feast of the Weeks. This is the day the church calls Pentecost and it is looked upon as the day when the Holy Spirit came to the disciples. Remember the saying about the Lord sending an angel. But in the original sense, Pentecost was observed to commemorate the gathering of the harvest. Later, it was associated with the giving of the laws on Mount Sinai.

However, it is the story of the Holy Spirit entering into the disciples that concerns us. Remember in the Bible Jesus promised to send a comforter and eventually that comforter came in the shape of the Holy Ghost or Holy Spirit. What puzzles us is who or what comforted the millions who lived before Jesus Christ was born or, more appropriately, died. As we understand it, the spirit enters our body before we are born. If it did not do so then we would not be living beings and that being so, what was it that came to the disciples at Pentecost? Was it the realisation that they were spirits in a material body rather than the other way round? Although the words are the same there is a large difference in the meanings because the emphasis in the first definition is on the spiritual.

Maybe this was the truth that came to the disciples for, from the evidence, we read in the bible they do not appear to have understood what Jesus meant when he said, at the feast of the Passover, 'Whither I go ye know and the way ye know.' We come to church each Sunday but do we understand what is being said and, more important, do we know the way? We ask this because there are people who attend churches of all religions who are more interested in material things than the spiritual.

When things go wrong we start blaming God and the spirit friends, saying that they have forgotten us, not realising that we are going along the wrong pathway and so have to be brought back on the right one. We are taught a lesson because that is what we are here for.

There was the man who followed spiritualism but, when he was taken ill and had to go to hospital, he became very bitter, saying that no medium had told him he would go to hospital. He did not seem to realise that, perhaps, his spirit friends were trying to protect him from too much trauma. What of the lady who called herself a spiritualist, who should have known that the passing of her daughter was a natural event because her daughter had gone to a higher school of learning. However, she became very bitter saying that there was no God, for he took her daughter and left rogues to carry on living.

Another man, a medium, crippled in his legs, ran a boarding house with his sister and was told clairaudiently that he had to get out. He went to see another medium who told him that the message was quite true to which he replied, 'But I am a spiritualist', thinking this made him something special. After a while he did move and some time later his sister passed away, thus proving that the spirit friends knew best because there was no way he could have managed the boarding house on his own.

Most people do not realise the power they bring with them when they are born into this earth plane but there are some who do and they use it in various ways. An older man, who in his younger days lived in a courtyard where there were several houses whose occupants would meet in one of the houses to use this power, told us that they had some wonderful experiences, which included the furniture floating about. But he also said, 'Of course we did not know what power we were playing with.'

Do we know what power is within us and do we realise that we have already experienced Pentecost when that power was given to us to make us living beings before we entered the earth plane? As Pentecost is associated with the laws, so is spiritualism. If we use the powers in the right way then we shall celebrate the harvest.

New Year

We stood tiptoe upon the mountain top of inspiration and for a moment looked on the future from the heights of high and glorious resolve but already this is beginning to fade. We are slipping back into our old ways and familiar ruts, we are becoming mentally lazy.

The Kingdom Within by Patience Strong

We are writing this early in the New Year but late enough for the festive season to be just a memory. Let us acknowledge that is what most of us think it is: a time for eating or drinking, a time for the giving and receiving of gifts and a time for sending greetings to people we will not give a thought to for the rest of the year.

The original story of Christmas is about God's gift to the world, a baby who, when he was born was hailed as King of the Jews, the prince of peace. Because of this we have at the festive season a message of peace and goodwill to all but, although this is observed for a short time, what happens afterwards? Remember the words we started with about the high resolve beginning to fade and as the feasting ends so the peace and goodwill begin to go. It shows that a lot of us do not know the true meaning of Christmas. Jesus was not born to be King of the Jews and more importantly he was not born and did not die so that our sins would be forgiven. We believe he was born into this earth to teach by living a spiritual life and to set an example on how we should live our lives. Now let us forget our New Year resolutions and concentrate on following that example.

Throughout the year all we seem to hear are moans and groans, gloom and doom. We must all take our share of the blame for this because we all do our share of the moaning. What we do not realise is that, by thinking pessimistically, we are drawing to ourselves that which is of the darker side of things. We grumble about the younger folk but, before criticising, let us consider who is responsible for the world into which they are born, who sets the examples for them to follow and who is responsible for their discipline? We hear of teachers being criticised because they are not doing this or they are doing that, but surely the teacher's job is to build on the foundation that should have been laid before they come into contact with the material they are supposed to mould. If there is no foundation then the structure will collapse and so we would ask, who is responsible for the structure? Therefore, before we start criticising other people's attitude and actions, let us be sure that our foundations are solid and will stand up to scrutiny.

In this New Year let us start by being optimistic and by looking for the good things in life because we will be surprised how many there are and in the most unlikely places. There are many people who do not go to church of any denomination and yet they are as spiritual and can converse about spiritual matters as well as someone who attends church every week. On two seperate occasions we met young men who not only had healing power, but were able to use it although they did not know where the power came from. These are the people who need guidance and, if we are able, we should give it.

Let our resolutions be that we are going to add something to life rather than taking something away, let us have positive thoughts rather than adopting a negative attitude. Do this by remembering that goodness spreads outwards like the ripples on a pond after a stone has been thrown into it, but let us also understand that badness also spreads inwards like a grub eating into an apple.

As we set out on our next voyage on life's ocean in the New Year, let God be our captain and spirits friends our crew. Let us put faith in them, accept their guidance because they too are on a voyage of progression. When we leave this earth let our epitaph be that we are a little richer and others have also gained because we passed this way.

Christmas and the New Year

We are now entering into another New Year, having just past the Christian festival of Christmas, when we celebrate or observe the birth of Jesus Christ, or do we?

What is our conception of Christmas, what does it mean to us and what does it mean to others? First and foremost, we think it means we are going to have a holiday with much feasting, eating, drinking and making merry. The season when we give away a lot of presents, wish people all the good things we can think of, peace on earth and goodwill to all men.

We read the story of Jesus and find that he was hailed the Prince of Peace and yet, looking through history, we find that much blood has been spilled in his name – quite a contradiction isn't it? However, in this season of goodwill, contradictions seem to play a large part because we give harmonious thoughts to all and sundry, even to those for whom we have not had a good word during the previous twelve months. Over the next few days we shall be wishing everyone 'A Happy New Year' and yet later, with the same tongue and from the same mouth, we shall be taking away their character.

During this holiday period we were drawn to two words, 'spirituality' and 'personality', to which we would add 'mortality', meaning materialism. In this sense materialism and mortality are things that do not last but eventually die. However, our personality and spirituality do not die because they are immortal but they can change, as we have shown through the examples given concerning the festive season.

Can we glance back over the last twelve months and look for any changes that may have taken place concerning ourselves during that period? Oh, we know we may have bought new furniture, new clothes, had alterations done to the house, even moved to a new house or job. But all these things are in a material sense and, as such, did not change our personality. Perhaps, at the time, we felt good inside but this is not our personality and we feel that the only thing that could change it is our spirituality, or lack of it.

Now we would ask you not to confuse the word 'spirituality' with the word 'spiritualist' because there are many who call themselves spiritualists who are not spiritual and, on the other side of the coin, there are those who have spirituality who want nothing to do with spiritualism. However, in both groups there are those who profess to be spiritually involved who, when the opportunity arises, are more interested in mortality. We can tell you of people who think they are good because they do not drink, do not smoke, do not gamble and do not buy newspapers or watch television on Sundays. Of course, when it is possible to make a quick penny or take advantage of their fellow men they are not slow in doing so and they are not particular on whom they trample to achieve their ends. Here again we have the contradictions we spoke of in regard to the festive season.

So what about spiritualists? You hear them say, 'I have been in the movement forty years', but you dare not ask them the obvious question, 'What have you learned in those forty years?' because you may embarrass them. What they mean is they have been coming to services forty years and have been receiving messages for that length of time but that is not spirituality. We do not know how long you have been attending but we hope that in the period you have, some knowledge and spirituality may have entered into your soul.

When we listen to the words the medium is saying we may not always agree with what he is saying but there could be one or two words which stick in our minds so let us use our thoughts and try to build something positive to help us spiritually. Let us try to find five minutes each day to sit, to close our eyes, to meditate, to reach out to the highest and gradually we will find we are receiving spirituality in return.

Through spirituality we shall develop tolerance to all with whom we come in contact, thus practising the brotherhood of man and peace on earth to all men.

The Way

'I am the way, the truth and the light.' As we talk among ourselves about our experiences through this the earthly part of our lives and the pathway we have taken because of those experiences, we should all pray that we may take the right paths for there are various ways we can go. Let us remember that we have free will so that we can choose our own pathway: no one forces us to do so or at least should not be allowed to.

There is the pathway of selfishness, of greed, the pathway of indifference and laziness. Of course, on the positive side, we can choose the pathway of sacrifice, of love, of guidance and, through these pathways, we find the way to inner peace and satisfaction.

'In my father's house are many mansions, I go to prepare a place for you and whither I go ye know and the way ye know', but do we know the way or are we like Thomas with our doubts? It was not the words that Jesus spoke that were important but the life he had led before those words. His life was the way and the words were the confirmation of that way.

When we enter into this world we have a choice and the choice allows us to forget that we came from a spiritual environment and therefore we are spirit. We can if we wish, and most of us do, realise that we have entered a material world and so become materialistic. Because of this attitude we go along the pathway we have chosen, picking the flowers from the wayside and helping ourselves to the fruit from the trees, without giving a thought to those who are following.

Maybe we fasten on to others, clinging to them, relying on them for assistance and using their energies to carry us along. Being indifferent, lazy and not endeavouring to help ourselves, by leaning, by trampling on others, we could find ourselves in a cul-de-sac having to retrace our steps. We could find that the flowers are fading, the fruit has lost its flavour and the taste has become bitter. This is when we realise that the riotous and selfish living has to stop so we pocket our pride and eat the husks that are fed to the pigs. We become as the prodigal son, saying, 'I will return to my father's house and ask to become one of his servants.'

When we think like this the light is beginning to pierce the gloom, we are starting to think in the right manner and our ideas and attitudes are beginning to change. We are turning to a spiritual way of thinking and remembering that we were spiritual, we are and always will be.

However, because we have changed our thinking and taken a new pathway, we should not expect the going to become easier, for the more sensitive we become to others the more difficult it will be to pass them by. What we will discover is that we are going somewhere, there will be no cul-de-sac and we will be going at a pace where we really appreciate the singing of the birds and seeing the true beauty of the hedgerows. We will enjoy the company of our fellow travellers, sharing in and enjoying their experiences.

So, when we meet the rough parts of our pathways, let us remember the compensations and that these rough parts are there as lessons so that we can progress further along the way. It is when we meet the rough parts that we have to put our trust in those spirit helpers but, at the same time, remembering that they can guide but cannot walk along the pathways for us. We have to have the rough parts so that we can appreciate the smoother stretches.

When we leave this earth plane, some parts of our journey will be rougher than others because we have to go through the mists, the valley of the shadows, before we can reach our cottage. It is probable that we will receive a good send-off with plenty of flowers but let us remember it is not the words we have spoken but how we have lived that matters. It is the way we have trod, the manner in which we have faced the truth that determines the amount of light that shines along the way on our journey.

6
Passing Over

When We Die

We have been asked on a number of occasions what happens to us when we die. In a couple of instances the inquirers seemed to be terrified as to what might happen to them if they don't wake up. This is misconception for eventually they will wake up.

However, as we are considered the experts in these matters we should be able to provide answers, but what sort of answers? It is no good telling them that they will go on living when they have attended funerals and seen bodies either burned or buried. It is like the little girl, who when taken to put flowers on her grandfather's grave posed the question, 'How can my grandad be down there if he is with Jesus?' Out of the minds of babes . . .

Again, it is no good saying that we shall have a life of ease with nothing to do except play musical instruments because there are thousands who have no musical talent and possibly no wish to acquire it. Furthermore we know several people who would be bored to death (if you will pardon the expression) with a life of ease. These are those who were always active, probably caring for others when here on the earth plane, and we don't think they are going to be happy or satisfied by just sitting back with nothing to do.

However, we are racing ahead and leaving our inquirers behind when we should be explaining that we all possess a spiritual body or soul as well as a physical one. It is the physical one which goes into the ground, or is burned, but the spiritual one lives on and so that is the answer to the little girl's question about her grandfather. The spirit is the living or activating part of us and without it we would be dead or at least our physical bodies would be. The spirit or soul is given to us by God and it is the only part that goes back from whence it came.

As we go back let us remember that we are making a return journey and the return should be easier and better than the initial. When we come to earth as babies we are the loneliest of creatures because the only person we have had any contact with is our mothers. However, during our stay on earth we become acquainted with other relatives and we also build up friendships so that when we return a lot of these people are waiting to meet and greet us.

Therefore the end of our journey, at least, will be more pleasant than the original one.

Can we explain it in the way we go or prepare to go on holiday? We travel to a strange place not knowing what to expect when we get there because we are going to stay with strangers and yet, at the end of the holiday, we find that we have had a good time with new friends. Maybe a better way to explain it would be to compare the experience of having to leave home to work in a distant part of the country or even abroad. When we go to these strange areas we are, at first, going to mix with strangers but eventually we form friendships. Of course, due to the circumstances, we cannot go home each night and have to keep in touch through letters or telephone until such time that we have finished our work. When we consider this, it is similar to the way in which our spiritual friends come back to say 'hello' to us and the way we will be able to come back when we have left this earth plane.

Let us at this point think of the children who come to this world and then are taken away from their parents in sad circumstances. On two separate occasions we were asked by mothers about their two small daughters. The first was concerned that her little girl would not know anyone in the place she had gone to but after telling her that the child must have known someone before leaving that place to come to earth the mother was more contented. The other mother was concerned that although she had been to spiritualist churches and had seen mediums and clairvoyants none had brought the child back to her, although one medium had told her that the child had passed away with a chest infection. This she agreed was true but she was unable to accept other things she was told. We advised her to go to a church where she was not known but we also told her there was no need for her to chase mediums because when the time was ripe and the child was able, she would make herself known to her mother. Remember that the bereaved one must be in the right frame of mind before contact can be made.

People say that it is a shame for babies because they do not ask to come into the world but we feel that this belief is wrong for babies *do* ask to come to earth and, furthermore, they even choose their parents. In the light of this we told the two mothers that they should feel proud to have been chosen to be parents. The babies probably had some experience to go through or some lessons to learn and these mothers were the most suitable to teach them. Therefore they should not grieve for them but feel elated that their children learned the lessons so quickly.

As we started out as babies this truth applies to us all because as we go to school and work in a material way so we have to learn lessons in a spiritual way. Let us remember that as we asked to come here originally we have committed ourselves to learn these lessons.

We should not have the belief that this part of our life is the be-all and end-all of our existence but think of it as the preparation for the real life which follows. This is why material wealth is of no use and, in fact, this wealth should be shared because only spiritual achievements count as collateral in the spiritual bank. Whatever spiritual achievements we make here through our endeavours determines the sort of dwelling and environment we have hereafter. Those who say eat, drink and be merry in the belief that there is nothing after this life will get just what they expect. Until they change their thoughts, and eventually they will, their states of darkness and inamination will remain with them but, when they realise what has happened to them, they will progress and make a future for themselves. This is what is meant by eternal progress open to every soul.

Let us realise that we all have the opportunity to progress remembering that we don't have to wait until we have passed from this world before learning our lessons. Of course we can sit back and do nothing but in the further life we will have many options open to us whereby we can follow interests that we may not have been able to when on earth.

Let us tell you of the lady who suffered all her life in a physical way through various ailments but she did not allow herself to become a martyr for she threw herself into helping others whom she thought were worse off than herself. After her passing one of her nieces went to see a medium who gave her name and said, 'She tells me it is lovely here and there is no pain.' We also have been given thoughts from this lady in which she made it known that she had met some of her loved ones and friends but also added that she had a nice garden which was one of her interests when here.

So you see there is nothing to be afraid of provided we believe that there is something after this life and there need be no pain or anguish if we build with spiritual bricks. We should not cause any anguish to those who have passed by grieving and crying because they have to progress and, when they see our tears, they want to be near us thus becoming distracted.

Nothing Ever Dies

Whilst we were talking once to a young lady the conversation somehow turned to the subject of death and she asked if we thought there was anything after this life because no one had ever come back to tell us. We told her not to be so sure because the latter part of her statement was debatable and we certainly thought that there was something afterwards. The young lady replied, 'You are probably right because nothing ever dies.' Oh, what words of wisdom.

Nothing ever dies although shapes may change from time to time, or season to season, and because the condition of form alters that does not mean death has taken place. Look at the trees in winter when to all intents and purposes they are dead but come the spring and we see new leaves beginning to form, whilst in the summer we see them in their full glory. With the arrival of autumn we see other changes when the leaves turn yellow, brown and gold.

We once moved a rose tree to another position in the garden and because it drooped after it was moved people said that it had died but as spring approached green shoots appeared on it and it has flowered ever since. Similarly we were told that the pear tree in our new garden was no good as it had not borne fruit for years but we got to work and pruned it severely and within two years the tree was loaded with fruit. Eventually we decided to get rid of it and so cut it down but could not remove all the roots and thereafter new shoots began to grow. You see whilst the roots are there nothing ever dies.

Let us consider the pruning of roses and other trees and bushes which is done to improve them in every way. Similarly, the disbudding or nipping of other flowers does not kill them but rather improves them. Things have to be controlled because if seeds are planted and left unattended, then we end up with a wilderness. This is how jungles are formed. While on the subject of planting seeds let us remember that after they have started to grow, we may have to 'thin them out' by transplanting them. This gives the plants a chance to breathe and grow.

If we compare ourselves with nature we can see the similarities because as we go through the seasons of our stay here so we experience changes. We have a physical body to enable us to live in this world but, as we progress from spring to winter, this body goes through many changes. Like the trees and plants our spring is a time of growing, of developing, of using the talents we have so that we can burst into full glory during our summer. This is followed by our autumn when we should be taking things easier and making the most of our experiences to be ready for our winter.

Of course, coming into a material world we are naturally drawn to that which is material, even from a very early age, because the example is put before us. Have you ever thought why we struggle to stay here when the future life is said to be so much better – could it be not only the material things that hold us back, but the love of them? Yet these are the things that fade away and die. This is the dead wood that has to be cut away because as we change physically so we have to change spiritually. It may come as a shock but there is quite a lot of pruning to be done. A great amount of disbudding has to take place if we want others to see our flowers and blooms in the best of condition.

Many things, which may have run wild previously, have to be controlled so that we do not have a jungle to hack our way through. Maybe we have to curb our tongues and tempers and thus learn tolerance; to stop thinking so much about ourselves by watering down our egos and thereby understanding humility; to listen to other people's problems, offer them advice and so find out what love and compassion is all about.

Sometimes we have to move away from the groups we have been associated with for lengthy periods because we have become stifled and are being bogged down. We have to transplant ourselves to be able to breathe or, to put it in another way, we have to seek fresh fields and new teachers so that we can progress. When we begin to do this we will understand more fully the purpose, the aim and the true meaning of life. As this becomes apparent we will know that we are learning lessons and shouldering our responsibilities. Above all, we will be able to say, 'Yes there is something after this life and I am looking forward to going there.'

Anything That Is Living Never Stands Still

Someone recently suggested that the gramophone was a good simile for life because we could be like the needle following the groove in the record. Just going round and round until we came to a scratch in the groove and then we would either jump over it or stop. We feel that rather than being in the groove we are in danger of being in a rut because, by just going round and round, we are showing that we have no ambition to lift ourselves above the scratches.

At about the same time as we heard the gramophone story, there was some correspondence in the local newspaper about a young couple who were expecting their first baby and were complaining that the council would not grant them the tenancy of a house. They had quite a number of replies asking why they were not doing something for themselves instead of sitting back waiting for others to do things for them. One letter was from a couple who had been in the same position as those who were complaining but they had tried to get a mortgage. However, the powers that be just laughed at their application because the husband was only a labourer and was not earning enough. They both went in to further education, made progress, improved their positions so that they were able to get off the turntable, out of the rut and into the groove.

It has been pointed out that with progress, the gramophone has become the record player and we do not even have to lift the needle off the record because it is done automatically. In fact some of these machines can play more than one record so that we find six and even ten records being placed on the turntable at the same time. As one record finishes so the next one drops into place and each one could have different songs, tunes and pieces of music with their varying moods.

What about us? Are we going to be like the gramophone record and wait to be lifted off the turntable? Are we going to be like the servant with one talent who buried it? On the other hand, we could have been fortunate enough to have taken our opportunities and made use of our talents.

As those long-playing records comprise various pieces of music with their different moods, so it is with our lives but we would call these moods 'cycles' and we should be able to learn lessons from them whether they be bright or dull. We go to church but why do we go? Is it because we want knowledge or do we go to get a message or, as some put it, 'to have our fortune told'? What of the message of philosophy and the lessons therein? If we can absorb these lessons then there will be no need for us to be lifted from the turntable.

You may be saying 'It is all right for him because he is a medium and can get his own messages' but this is not quite so. Mediums do not get messages in the usual way but, by having trust and faith in their guides, they know that even if they have to tread a road they would rather avoid, they will arrive at the right destination.

Of course, to get to this stage we have to be patient, possibly change our attitudes to life and above all develop spiritual gifts. This cannot be achieved by coming to church each Sunday to listen to various speakers but to forget everything that has been said when we leave. If we can remember one sentence or phrase it will be something to start our thought working and let us remember that our thoughts are something that can never die.

We once sat in a circle in which a young man was a member and he came up one evening to ask how he could develop a little more quickly, so we pointed out to him that he was coming one week and missing two or three. Perhaps the guides and helpers did not think he was steadfast enough to be persevered with. It is no good stopping the record half-way through if we want to hear the full piece of music. We cannot stop life half-way through because it is always alive, it cannot die so let our purpose be to progress – let us give it a try.

Suicide

When man is born into the earth plane he brings with him a free will which, it is said, makes him different and also of a higher intelligence than other animals. How much leeway does this free will give mankind?

We ask this because of two or three things that have occurred. Firstly, sometime ago, we were asked what was the spiritualists' viewpoint concerning suicide. A lady had come to us to say that a friend of hers had taken her own life and she wondered how she would fare. Secondly, some days later, there was a television programme called *A Right To Live and a Right To Die*. Lastly, we have people who are always calling for the return of capital punishment.

In the light of these happenings we ask, has man any right in the matter of life or death? If so, how much right has he or should he take? Remember, as spiritualists, we believe that all living creatures, including animals, have souls or spirit bodies.

If one of our pets is suffering we have it 'put to sleep' because we consider it wicked to allow it to suffer. So we take the decision that says we have the right to say they must die. If we consider we have this right concerning animals, what about the decision when it involves human beings? They too, like animals, have souls but they have something extra – they have free will, so they can decide for themselves. However, what about those whose condition is such that they cannot make that decision? Those who we say, rather unkindly, they are no more than vegetables and that they are being kept alive by being connected to machinery of all kinds. Have we a right over their living or dying? Can we switch off those machines knowing that we are doing the right thing?

Someone said there is only one authority that has the power to take that decision. Remember these people have souls and until that authority takes those souls to another place they are living things, or are they? If we switch off these machines are we guilty of murder? We will come back to this later.

Which brings us back, conveniently, to capital punishment. When someone is sentenced to death there is a period of time between the sentence and the carrying out of it. During this time the condemned person has time to think and more importantly to brood over many things, not least vengeful thoughts. As life is continuous, these thoughts are taken into the further life and thoughts being living things they can come back to influence others on the earth plane.

You ask, 'What about the victims?' Here we feel we have a different situation because the victims pass quickly and therefore do not take vengeful thoughts with them and so are receptive to the ministrations that are given to them by those experienced in such matters.

On the other hand, the condemned person's mind is in such a state that he is not receptive to these ministrations. Someone who has been reprieved has the opportunity to be taught differently and so get rid of his vengeful thoughts.

Back to those who are lying on beds of sickness in terrible pain and asking why God has forsaken them. These people probably wish to get rid of their material bodies in the belief that they are not going to recover. How often has it been said that they are rambling or delirious but have we considered that they are already half-way to the spirit world and they are not talking to us at all but to those they knew in their earlier days? They could have come to the realisation that their physical bodies are no longer any good to them and so they want to get rid of them.

No matter how we go from this earth nothing will change and we will find we are still on the pathways we are supposed to be following, so if we take our own lives, we have not altered anything and we have not dodged our responsibilities. All we have done is to get rid of our physical overcoats. The pressures we could not face on the earth plane we shall still have to face in the hereafter and we still have the same goal to reach. May the divine spirit help us.

Evil Spirits

Each week we attend church to listen to different speakers and to hear readings from various books and, although we do not always agree with what we hear, there is on occasion a phrase which sets us thinking. This chapter is about one of those occasions.

In a reading we heard recently were the words: 'The mind of man is the manifestation of the spirit within him and as this spirit is akin to the divine spirit the human mind must have some relationship with God'. To us this means that if God is all goodness, then there must be some goodness in us all. Following this reading, the medium said that the man in the street did not understand spiritual things and went on to speak not only of spiritual things but also of emotional.

We bring these things to mind because we have heard so much recently about evil spirits and exorcism, even reading of one classic example about a man who had twenty-four evil spirits cast out of him. It makes one wonder how they all got into him in the first place. Of course, anything to do with spirits (except in a bottle) and spiritualism frightens people. A lady told a friend that she was scared stiff of anything to do with spiritualism. Now this lady knows me and thinks I am a normal, reasonable fellow. But she does not know that I am a spiritualist. The query is raised: would her attitude change if she did know?

We once gave a message to a man in church but could make no headway with him and when we spoke to him after the service he told us that he was scared stiff. Then there was the young lady who asked for advice because she said a gypsy had put a curse on her, so we had to tell her that no one could do this to anyone unless the person was so weak willed as to think that it could happen and then it would be something to do with emotion rather than spiritualism.

My wife was speaking to two young ladies and they asked if I was a spiritual medium and on being told 'Yes' they said they wanted nothing to do with me. The young ladies said that they knew someone who had been to a spiritualist church and ever since they 'have had a ghost' in the house. It was probably Uncle Bill or

Auntie Mary who had come to visit them because they had shown an interest by going to the spiritualist church.

These are the sort of things that can happen and, because people do not understand them, they become frightened and think something evil is taking place. We have only to look back in history for proof because when anyone showed mediumistic powers they were shunned and even burned at the stake, even though they may have performed what was looked upon as a miracle.

Someone recently remarked that the world wanted someone to come along and perform something spectacular but haven't we just shown what would happen if they did? If nothing violent occurred, people would say, 'What is the trick or where is the catch?'

Once we saw a programme on television about healing in which the presenters proved that it was trickery and nothing but a fake. The sick went to the healers on a wave of emotion but came back with no cure. One lady said that she was convinced that she had been cured but the medical authorities said they could find no change in her condition. What had happened was the lady had been carried along on a wave of emotion that uplifted her so much that she thought she was cured.

We know a gentleman who is a hypnotherapist and he did the same for a young lady with an incurable disease by making her a musical tape. The young lady said that when she played the tape she felt better, but she was never cured. This is no criticism of the gentleman because he knew the lady would not recover and did not promise a cure but he knew that the tape would be of benefit.

We worked with someone who became involved with a religious group, so much so that he was full of it and it became his life. One day he came to work and put a notice on the board advertising a healing meeting to be conducted by an evangelist minister. A workmate took his son to see if the healing would improve the boy's eyes. When asked how things had gone he replied, 'I am afraid it wasn't my scene at all, it was too emotional.' This is our way of thinking because we feel that all healing should be done quietly and as privately as possible.

In a similar way, people seek advice and so they start to experiment with the ouija board but this is the wrong way to get advice. Some of those people who take part in the experiments could be of an emotional nature and something could be spelt out that plays on their minds so that they become ill with worry. Because of this we are told by the so-called experts that they have been taken over by evil spirits when, in actual fact, it is their own emotions and nerves that have made them ill.

Now who determines what an evil spirit is? Let us remember the words of the reading that spirits are all related to God, so there is some good in us all. We feel a better phrase would be 'undeveloped' or 'uneducated spirits.' We have the same thing in our material world with people who have not been very well educated. At one period of our working life we met people who were seeking employment and on one occasion we had to complete a man's application form because he could not read or write. Sometime later we met the man's supervisor who told us what a good worker he was, saying, 'I can give him a job, leave him and when I come back I know the work will be done.' There we have an uneducated, undeveloped man and yet someone found him useful. It is the same with undeveloped spirits for once someone shows an interest in them, in the right way, then they can become useful.

However, we are told that only the experts should deal with them by exorcising them. The experts being the bishops and the clergymen, who tell spiritualists not to meddle with the dead. No sincere spiritualist would even try. Do these experts, who cast out devils, work in a proper manner? Do they realise that not only those who are possessed but also those doing the possessing are sick? The possessed do not want to be shaken to death or to be screamed and shouted at in the manner that the experts work. More likely they need love, compassion and kindly words of advice.

That is what everyone will get if they have sincere thoughts and good intentions. We can all come to church, get healing, guidance and we can also send our thoughts to the church thereby receiving some of the power that has accumulated therein.

Remember, however, we will get only what we pay for so, if we want sensationalism, then we could get a shock and find our hopes and ambitions being burned at the stake.

Death

For some years now we have to visit hospital periodically for a check up but, as the years have passed, we are glad to say that the visits have become fewer. All those attending this clinic were on a diet of some description and, on one occasion while waiting to see the doctor, we sat next to two ladies who were rather perturbed about gaining weight since their last visit.

One of the ladies said that she knew that she could lose weight but she liked a good life and good food too much to be able to do so. In saying this the lady showed that she hadn't the will-power or resolution to make the effort. The other lady said that her illness ran in both her own family and that of her husband so she felt it was impossible to keep her weight down. She then mentioned that two of her relatives had died as a result.

At this point the first lady said, 'Oh, don't let us talk about death, I am enjoying life too much to think about dying.' However, the other lady replied that we all had to die some time and referred to plants and flowers and how they just faded and died. They then turned to me and asked what I thought about dying to which I replied that if I had no responsibilities I was ready to go tomorrow because we were always being told that the next place was better than this one.

The retort came immediately: 'Oh yes, but is there another place because when you are dead that is the end with nothing to follow?' The one lady said she knew this was so because when she suffered a heart attack she had 'died' and there was nothing but darkness. Now we know another lady who had the same experience, including the darkness, but she also saw a light as if she was in a tunnel. This lady said that if she had reached that light no one and nothing would or could have brought her back. We feel that both these ladies experienced the valley of the shadows. However the thought strikes us – if the first lady was dead and done with, how did she come to be sitting there telling us about her experiences? Unfortunately, at this point, we were called to see the doctor and so were unable to continue the discussion which we thought could have become very interesting especially when linking it with some words we had read before going to the hospital: 'The truth about death.'

Now various people have differing views about death and we have just mentioned one, so who can tell us the truth about it? We have those who become very sorrowful and wear nothing but black clothing with no other colour to take away the darkness. Another group hold some sort of celebration. A lady passed away and her famous son said, 'For myself I am shattered but for my mother I am very pleased.' Another young lady was killed in a motor accident and her parents requested 'no flowers' and would not close the curtains as a sign of mourning because they did not want their daughter's soul impeded on its journey.

So throughout the world there are various customs which may be strange to us but not to those who believe in them, so let us remember that not everyone shares our beliefs. However, we do find some curious contradictions, such as a family who do not believe that there is anything after death but when a loved one is dying send out a wish that someone will come to fetch them. We remember a lady, whose husband had suffered ill health for many years and who had once again taken to his bed in a serious condition, calling out, 'Oh Lord, take him.' Some time after he had passed, perhaps when feeling sorry for herself and having a little moan, she was reminded that she had asked God to take him.

Now we are convinced of life after death because of the things that are given to us and also the loved ones that we have brought back to others. However, we sometimes come across things that puzzle us. One occasion was when we told a lady of the little Japanese guide standing behind her who was crying but she was not to worry as they were tears of joy. Imagine our feelings when within a month we were told that this lady's husband was seriously ill in hospital and that not long afterwards that he had passed away. We pondered long and very deeply over this and wondered whether we had read the symbols wrongly or whether the tears of joy were from those in spirit because they were welcoming back a friend? When we come into this world there is rejoicing and when we leave it there are tears and sadness. Does the same thing happen in the spirit world so that they are sad when someone leaves to come to the earth plane but they are happy on their return? It is worth giving it some thought.

The fact that we have written and you are reading this book shows that we have some knowledge of life after death and that we have absorbed some teachings but not everyone has, even some of those who attend spiritual churches. Let us go back to the lady who would not keep to her diet because she liked good food. In following this policy she did not realise the food that she was eating was poisoning her body. She could have enjoyed good food but it could have been the right type and it could have kept her healthy.

It is the same spiritually when people will not take the right spiritual food because it would mean making sacrifices and so they will not adopt the right thoughts and attitudes. The people who wear black as a sign of mourning are only drawing darkness around themselves which in turn brings dark thoughts. Let us break away from these things by having bright and positive thoughts.

What about the statement about the plants having their day and then dying? We know they flower and then appear to fade away but after a season they reappear in all their glory. This is what happens to us when after our season here we are called to bloom in another garden. We are here to be educated in the way of life, the true way and the true life, and when we have learned those lessons we move on to another school. Surely when a loved one leaves this school of learning we should rejoice that they have progressed to the next stage of their education in the same way that we are happy for someone who advances to university here on the earth plane.

World of Illusion

In one of our addresses we made the remark that this was a world of illusion and the next was the real world. To us this was quite an innocent observation but it created a lot of discussion after we had left the church. In the light of these events, will you share with me a few thoughts as we examine the remark. First let us determine what illusion is. The dictionary says it is 'delusion, deception and having false beliefs.'

All religions teach that there is a life after death even though they may have different ideas about how it is going to be achieved. Although they have differing beliefs or creeds, they are in agreement on one thing and that is – life is continuous. At this point we should ask how many people believe this when we hear so many say, 'When you are dead you are finished', thereby saying there is no such thing as life after death. These people are deluding themselves because when they leave this world they will experience nothing but darkness until they realise they are still living and then they will make progress.

We are also taught that we not only have a physical body but also a spiritual one, which people call a soul. Most people talk about the soul in common-enough phrases such as, 'body and soul' or 'poor old soul' but how many know what the soul is? Without it we would not be living beings because it is the animating part of man. For those who say they haven't one we can only say that they are suffering from a delusion. These who say that when you are dead you are finished cannot recognise they have a soul for it is the only part that lives on.

The Bible tells us the story of the resurrection of Jesus and we read that when those who went to the tomb early on that morning they discovered the stone rolled away and the body missing. Because of this account we feel that many people have been misled and deluded into thinking it was the physical body that left this world. This is one very strong reason why people feel that if their body is buried or burned, it cannot, or rather they cannot, go to another world.

We must not suffer from the illusion that what we are experiencing in this world is the beginning of our lives, for those lives began in another world before we came here and we shall return to that world when we leave this one. The other world was lighter, brighter and finer than this one with none of the solid atmosphere we have here. In that world we were sheltered. Therefore the life we are now experiencing is a challenge, a testing time to see how we cope with the baser materials and atmosphere of earth. Without experiencing these things how can we help others, after we have gone, when they call out to us while they are going through the trials and traumas we have experienced?

When we say that we come into this world, we should explain that our souls enter into a physical body before it is born and it is the soul that makes the baby into a living thing. Here is another illusion because a lot of people consider the physical body as the most important, when without the spiritual it would be dead.

Besides the soul we have every emotion we can think of whether it is good or bad, for we must have positive and negative in everything. Man is also given a free will so he can use his emotions as he wishes and that is why we find such things as jealousy, envy, greed, lust which leads on to other things like cruelty, murder, bloodshed, muggings and even war. The challenge of this world is to see how we deal with our emotions and free will but we must remember we shall have to go back to the real world to see the exam results.

Something else we all possess is a conscience, a safety valve which helps us to measure standards and tells us what is right and wrong.

In the light of what we have just mentioned we suppose that, according to our standards, the emotions we have spoken about are wicked but do those who use them feel the same? Do they, because they have the strength and power, feel they have the right to impose their wills on others to obtain more power?

However, let us all ask ourselves another question – do these emotions and actions take place in the spirit world? Surely the answer must be no. So who is suffering from illusions by having false beliefs in thinking that the power they misuse here is going to help them in the hereafter?

Let us take the example of those who strive to make fortunes through material wealth in this world but when they die they have to leave it all behind because it is of no use to them. We have all heard the saying 'You can't take it with you', and it is quite true because it will buy nothing in the next phase of life. Another form of wealth and power is needed in the next world and that is why they have to change their thoughts, ideas and actions. They will then realise that previously it was all illusion.

We sing a hymn in which are the words, 'We give thee back the life we owe that in thine ocean depths its flow may richer fuller be.' The reason we are here is that our souls may be richer and fuller because of the experience we have gone through and that we may be able to leave a little piece of the reality of the spirit world upon this planet of illusion.

7
Omega to Alpha

I or We

I am George Knight but of course you know that because you have seen my name on the front of this book. A name is something we are given when we are born so that people can identify us. In fact without one we would be lost because there are so many forms and papers which are issued by various authorities that without names no information would be gathered. Even our pets are named so that we do not have to say, 'Come here cat' or 'come here dog', because if we had more than one cat or dog, we would be in trouble. Similarly, if we had to call everyone 'man' or 'woman' we would be in the same predicament.

When we cannot remember a name we have to resort to descriptions, sometimes physical but other times going a little deeper. By this we mean describing someone as a 'quiet sort of person who stays in the back ground but if there was any help needed they would always be there to give it'. Again we cannot go round describing people, so we use names and this is the only reason that they are important.

I have told you who I am but that is not important, but what I am *is* and the same applies to you. Sometime ago we were asked if we could write a few words about healing and guides, mentioning the guides names, but here we were stumped because we could not name one guide who was associated with me.

Many years ago, when we first entered into spiritualism, we became interested in healing and so started to develop the gift but, as we progressed, other gifts became apparent so that philosophy was absorbed and clairvoyance came to the forefront. Due to this and on other people's recommendations, we visited other churches, thus it was that George Knight became known to quite a number of people in various districts. We presume that if we had stayed fully and solely involved with healing at one church we would not have been so well known, if at all.

Often, after we have taken a service, someone will come to tell us that a particular guide has been with us and then proceed to give a description of the guide. Now we know these guides help us and will continue to do so – they are even here now but, despite this, we cannot give you a name that would identify them.

Perhaps like me they do not think names are important but it is *what* they are and what they can do that really matters. We may not know that they are there, similar to the person we mentioned before who stands in the background but steps forward when needed. When needed the guides step forward. This is what healing is all about – something that is done quietly and the more quietly, the more efficiently. . . . Let us remember that any guides that come along are specialists in their field and they come not only so that they can pass their knowledge on to us but also because they, too, are desirous of progressing.

So we ask not who we are but what we are and what we can do because of what we are. The answer is that we are part of a great power, a living power from where we get all our energies and without this power we would be dead. That is why there is no such thing as death because this power never has and never will die. Being part of this power, we too can never die.

The guides and helpers that we have been describing of have lived upon this earth in physical form and although they have departed from earth, they still live on because they are part of this power. Therefore, when they come back to work with us as a team and we talk of our spiritual achievements, let us use the word 'we' and not 'I'. Remember the guides have had more experience and are therefore qualified to teach. Too many people, including mediums, think they are the important ones but, without the guides and the power, they would be nothing.

Examine Ourselves

We suppose we all look in the mirror everyday and we would say that those who do not must be very conceited. However, when we do look, do we like what we see? This question is posed because of a letter that was printed in a newspaper in which the writer said that one of her grandmother's sayings was, 'Of all the things we wear, our expression is the most important'.

It would be a good thing if our friends and acquaintances told us what we really looked like, in the manner of the little girl who said to someone, 'Look at the state of your face.' We wonder what she could see but, more important, what did she mean? Remember the words of Robert Burns – 'Oh to have the gift to see ourselves as others see us', and consider the amount of worry and trouble that could be prevented if it were possible.

Sometimes in our prayers we mention the puzzles and perplexities of life asking that we may receive guidance to solve these things. We have no doubt that we receive the guidance but do we act upon it or even give it any thought? In the majority of cases we would say no because we want someone else to solve them and so those puzzles and perplexities are blamed for many things but rarely blamed is the real reason – ourselves.

We grumble about our conditions, envying others who seem to have progressed more than us and it is then that we become jealous thus creating discontent within ourselves. We listen to what others have to say and a lot of it is rumour and scandal but nevertheless it makes us dissatisfied. Here is an example: – at the place where we used to work, one of the groups of people were granted certain privileges and immediately the cry went up from the others, 'What about us?' All sorts of moaning and groaning went on but not a thought about whether they were worthy of privileges themselves. At the time we said that we were trying to shut our ears and mind to all the talk that was going on because we did not want to become discontented. Let us have the understanding that we create things in this world, whether they are good or bad and we are the only ones that can change these things.

We go on holiday, enjoy ourselves and have a good time but then we have to return home so that we can go back to work. People ask what sort of holiday we have had and we say it was great until we had to 'come back to this God-forsaken hole'. Is it any wonder that it is God-forsaken when we have no charitable thoughts – remembering that thoughts are living things. We know a young man who is quite well to do and comfortably off in a material sense because he has worked very hard to achieve this but recently he received a jolt which slowed him down. He realises that this could have been the best thing to have happened because he was probably heading for a breakdown but his mind is still in a turmoil. This is due to the fact that he cannot proceed with his plans as fast as he would wish and so his mind is still unsettled. This is what we mean when we say we become discontented. Let us count our blessings in that we have work to go to and have the health and strength to do that work.

Maybe we are at loggerheads with someone of our acquaintance, even in our own family, saying that he or she is being stubborn by not accepting our argument or seeing our point of view. Just a moment – let us ponder and ask if we want to understand another point of view. We could feel wronged and so want revenge but if this thought is uppermost in our minds then it is wrong and we need to look closely in the mirror.

There was a programme on television about prisoners in jail who had been taking part in an experiment to fit them for life after they had been released. One man who was interviewed said, 'I used to blame the circumstances but now I understand it is the way I dealt with them.' From personal experience we know that this is true so, instead of flying off the handle, we should remain calm, listen to the other point of view and we will find that things drop into place more easily, giving us peace of mind.

A lady was talking about retirement: she said it gives us a chance to look back and it is not all goodness that we see. Let us look deeper, look closer into the mirror and see where we are going wrong before it is too late. Let us realise that there are still things to be done and time is running out.

We must also understand that we are not the only ones who are doing the examining because those departed loved ones who come to guide us are also looking closely at us. When we join them we shall have to look at a large television screen that will hide nothing and then we will see ourselves as we really are.

Personality

Looking back through history we find men and women who may have inspired others with their words but perhaps did even more so by their actions and examples.

We think of Buddha and the way he sought something he could believe in before spreading his teachings to others; of Joan of Arc with her sacrifices; of St Francis of Assisi and his compassion for animals. Coming nearer to today and perhaps in a more material sense, we think of Adolph Hitler, with his ability to draw thousands to him through his speeches; of Winston Churchill, who inspired people to great efforts through his phraseology during the war. What of the church leader, Dick Sheppard, who, during the war drew crowds to him in the open air with his plain words and simple language?

All these people had one thing in common in that they were able to draw others to them and to persuade them to follow their teachings but they were also people who could fade from memory, living only in history books. There is one history book today which tells of a man who was able to draw others to him, who has not been forgotten: schoolchildren know of him even though he died nearly two thousand years ago. Why is this? Did he have qualities that others did not have? After all he was not an educated man and yet they came to be healed, they came to be comforted, they came to be taught and to gain knowledge of life itself. They knew he did things that were considered impossible like turning water into wine or healing someone who touched the hem of his clothing. Children surrounded him and in fact all types of people came to him.

Here was a humble man born into humble circumstances in a place called Bethlehem which, even in those days, when the world was so much smaller, was not very well known. In spite of his humble beginning, he is not forgotten and in fact he has made his birthplace and the other places he visited famous. Well we have tried to show that Jesus was no different to us and maybe not so educated as the majority of today, so the quality we are looking for cannot be material and therefore it must be spiritual. A man with such qualities must have lived very close to the spiritual world. When examining any situation we feel he would have looked at it from a spiritual viewpoint whereas we, being more materially minded, would look at things in a material way.

This is why some of these other people we mentioned tend to be forgotten because anything appertaining to the material has to fade away and die but spiritual things are indestructible and last or live for ever.

If we try to cultivate spiritual gifts and follow a spiritual way of life we have eventually to change our attitude. This is how Jesus was and he must have sacrificed a lot of his time to develop that spirituality because he only had to look at people to make them feel spiritual. Remember the story of when he told the disciples to take off their shoes for they were standing on holy ground, although it was just a piece of ordinary earth but, because of the spiritual power, it became consecrated. Jesus taught that you could pray or worship anywhere, in the open air, in our own homes, in small rooms and yet, despite his teachings, we find leaders of religions have built great edifices in which to worship. This may be all right but we feel that at times the building becomes more important than the teachings.

Our opinion is that Jesus was put to death because people did not understand his personality and they had their priorities wrong. When he rode into Jerusalem they thought he had come to free them from the bondage of the Romans when, in fact, he came to tell them how to release themselves from the narrow concept of the material bindings. After mixing with them, after talking to them, they still did not recognise he was showing them a new way of life. Let us get our priorities right by turning to the simple things, the natural things, the spiritual things.

Jesus was not a priest or some great church dignitary, so let us remember he was no different to us and most likely did not get such a good material start. Let us follow his example in everything. We do not need a first-class education or great learning because our spirit friends will teach us and let us remember some of the greatest mediums were very poorly educated.

Music

We would like to begin by telling you of the lady who travelled into the city by bus and throughout the whole journey a man was playing a mouth organ. As she left the bus, she turned and said to him, 'Thank you very much, that was beautiful.'

The man replied, 'Yes, missus, we have to have music. We can't do without it.'

Here we have a man, perhaps, not so wholesome in appearance, who had something that was beautiful but, more important, he was willing to share it with others.

What about music and pleasure as it affects us? We may think we are small and of no consequence but we feel that it is the small things in life that give most pleasure. Like the smile of a child as it runs towards you and throws its arms around your neck. We remember sitting in the car, with the window down, waiting for the traffic lights to change when suddenly we heard a child's voice coming through the air, 'Uncle George, Uncle George.' We turned our head and on the opposite pavement stood a little girl whom we had met on two or three occasions previously. She was bursting her lungs so that we could hear her and when we acknowledged her, she beamed all over her face. We felt like a millionaire because we had been adopted.

Then there was the little girl, aged six or seven, who for over an hour, gave an almost word-for-word performance of *The Sound of Music* to a group of people and thus brought pleasure to those folk. In fact, one lady was wiping her eyes for most of the performance. Not with sorrow but with joy. We give these examples because they may be small things concerning small people but they gave pleasure to others. The man on the bus did not warrant a second look but he gave upliftment to those around him so, no matter how small we feel, let us remember we can still play a part in helping others.

Consider the workings of a watch, how small and even minute they are and yet when they are assembled they all play their part in a successful piece of mechanism. However, if one of these small parts goes wrong, the watch ceases to function. It only needs one instrument to be out of tune and the whole orchestra sounds terrible. It can be likened to a well-knit family: when one of its members is not there the wheels do not run so smoothly. With the absence of that one instrument the family orchestra is out of tune.

As we travel around the different churches, we like to think that we are visiting families but if there has been any trouble in the church then the music does not sound so sweet. We remember one church we visited where there was always a harmonious atmosphere but on our last visit there seemed to be, shall we say, an undercurrent. We discovered later that there had been a difference of opinion and someone was showing and feeling resentment. It certainly spoiled the music. At another church was a man who was a real livewire, a go-getter and someone who had put all his energies into making the church successful. If he was not the conductor he was certainly the leader of the orchestra but, after he had retired, the church did not seem to be the same.

This shows a fault in the system, because everything seemed to be left to this one man and no one was ready to take his place. When someone leaves the orchestra someone else should be able to step into his or her shoes and this is where developing circles play their part. People should be trained in the various gifts of clairvoyance, healing, philosophy but, above all, told about the truths as shown in the principles of spiritualism. Young people should be accepted on to church committees, taught how to play various instruments so that they will know something about church procedure and be ready to take another's place when he retires.

Coming to church on Sundays does not give us the right to call ourselves spiritualists and if we think it does then we are really out of tune. The thing that matters is what we do for the rest of the week and what sort of tune we play then. This will determine what sort of orchestra we play in.

What we learn in church on Sundays from various speakers must be practised during the week. When we take music lessons in a material way we have to pay and the lessons may only last for thirty minutes but the important part is putting into practice what we have learned during those thirty minutes. We may be able to read the notes but we must practise so that those notes sound like a melody.

We have met many people who are equipped to play in a spiritual orchestra but will not practise or teach others. Do not make the mistake by being the player who is out of tune.

Ships Passing

We were once asked if it was possible to arrange coach trips to other churches and spiritualist associations. This we attempted to do but circumstances were such that we had to approach other people at different churches in the neighbourhood so that eventually groups from other areas became involved.

The first trip was such a success that each year we were asked if I would organise another and in fact some would ask, as they were getting off the coach, 'Where are we going next year?' Through these visits we have been privileged to meet wonderful and interesting people in all parts of the country. Then, when we go to speak at the local churches, we meet those who have been on the trips – our fellow travellers.

This phrase made us think because aren't we all fellow travellers on life's highway, going towards the same place? Maybe we are taking different routes, have differing beliefs and varying means or methods of getting there. We are of different creeds, different colours, from different nations with differing cultures and because of this we have upsets and disputes. We believe our way is better than any one else's but, by adopting this attitude, we become dogmatic and thus we can cause a lot of antagonism, which can result in disputes.

We have recently met someone who is very much involved with spiritualism, so much so that he is very dogmatic in his points of view. Unfortunately, he does not want to consider any thoughts or ideas put forward by others. To us this attitude is wrong because by showing tolerance to others and listening to them we can all learn something and make progress.

After we had taken a church service a young man approached us to ask us how and where he could develop spiritually. We invited him home for a chat to see if he would fit in with the group we had just started. We only knew him as Mark but after a couple of weeks we discovered that we had known his father, twenty years previously. Because of this something puzzled us and so we asked the question, 'As your father was so involved with spiritualism, why have you only just become interested?' His reply was that his father does not ram his views down other people's throats but if they showed an interest he would have a discussion. All this seemed to be confirmed when we later met his sisters who were also beginning to investigate spiritualism.

This brings us to a young man who came to see us on a business matter and the talk turned to cars, hobbies and interests. When he asked if we had any interests we said that we had one but did not think it was one in which he would become involved. As he insisted that we tell him something about it we said that it concerned spiritual matters and immediately the conversation dried up. If the young man had wanted to, we would have talked all night but we do not believe in casting pearls before swine.

You see man has been able to discover, invent and make wonderful things like ships, planes, computers and many labour-saving devices, but he has not yet discovered how to use his leisure time in a useful way. Of course he has made progress in other ways because today little boys do not have to go up chimneys.

This reminds us of the man who was arguing with his manager about working conditions when the manager said, 'Jack, you are always wanting something improved.' Jack replied, 'Years ago children were sent down pits and were more expendable than the ponies with whom they were working. Things have changed and I would like those who follow me to find further improvements. That the world will be a better place because I have walked on it.' So say us all.

A lady we once knew had just retired after working for the same company for thirty years and she said the thing that had made her mad was people saying she had not changed in all that time. She said she must have been an old-looking twenty-eight or a young-looking fifty-eight. I would have been mad as well but not for reasons of looks or beauty. If people had said that I had not changed in thirty years, I would have been very upset and disappointed. It would have meant that I had not progressed, not mellowed, had not matured and had not fulfilled the purpose of my being on earth. That would have meant that I had not become educated in spiritual matters or begun to understand the meaning of life. Let us hope that others can see changes in us all.

We hope that as we have journeyed across the ocean of life our fellow travellers will have learned something from us and we have been taught something by them through persuasion and example, not by force. When they send out a cry for help let us be ready to go to the rescue, for we never know when *we* may have to send out a SOS signal.

Man is born into this world for a reason and he has to work out his own destiny so if we try to change his pathway against his will we are upsetting that destiny and interfering with his karma. Let us influence him by our spiritual way of living, always remembering that one day we shall all meet again.

Holidays

We hear people say that there is no need for them to go to church because they are and can be as good as those who do go. Maybe this is so. However, we would like to ask these same people if they ever go on holiday and, if so, why? Their answer would probably be, 'Oh, for a change or a rest and to get away from it all.' When they say 'getting away from it all' they mean getting away from the humdrum things of life, the things they do everyday, the things that tend to become monotonous.

So they go away to get some good clean air into their lungs and, let's face it, most of us who live in industrial areas are glad to get away so that we can breathe some clean air instead of the usual smog. Of course all the arrangements have to be sorted out beforehand with the decisions of where we are going, our accommodation, how we shall travel and by which route. Some people like to go to luxury hotels with their services and entertainment whilst others prefer smaller, homely places with personal services. Yet again we have those who prefer do-it-yourself holidays: staying in caravans, flatlets, holiday villas or bungalows doing their own cooking and catering. Whichever way it is, the change has done us some good and we feel better for being away from it all.

To have a good holiday, it helps to have fine weather because there is nothing more miserable than watching the rain tumbling down when we are away from home and it is a lot worse when children are involved. We know of one man who says that the sun must shine everyday before he will say he has had a good holiday which we think is asking a lot. There are some people who cannot take too much sunshine. Another acquaintance used to go to the same place every year until one year someone gave him an invitation to stay with them which he accepted and he was agreeably surprised at the difference in this new type of holiday. So much so that he remarked that his usual place had had it as far as he was concerned.

Now we read in the Bible that Jesus withdrew, on a number of occasions, to seek rest, peace and inspiration. Rest for the physical body, peace for the mind and inspiration for the spirit. Mary and Martha tended to his needs, even to the washing of his feet and, on another occasion, he fell asleep on board a ship, thus resting his mind. We are reminded of the time he took the disciples up the mountainside and told them to take off their shoes because they were standing on holy ground, but they did not understand what he meant. We read that they fell asleep but we feel that they went into trance so that they could create the power for Jesus to communicate with the spirit guides.

It is this power that we come to church to find, the power that will lift us from the humdrum things of life in the material sense, the power that is the sunshine breaking through the clouds. There are times when we are at our wits end or down in the dumps, so we come to church to see if we can get some fresh thoughts into our minds in the same way that we go on holiday to get some fresh air into our lungs.

So we decide to go to church, but which one? Do we want something large and glorious with all the pomp and ceremony similar to the large luxurious hotels that some holidaymakers use? Maybe we would prefer something smaller, something more homely where we can relax and understand what is taking place. Of course, like do-it-yourself holidays, we could find a place where we could take an active part in the proceedings.

These observations apply to all denominations and not just to spiritualism. We must realise that some religions are very strict in their beliefs and the followers of those religions must do as they are told and follow those beliefs blindly without asking questions. We knew of one lady who left one religion and entered the spiritualist church because when she asked questions at her original church no one could or would give satisfactory answers. She found the answers in spiritualism and eventually became a medium.

Not everyone, however, is like that lady for many are willing to believe everything they are told, will follow blindly and defend their beliefs to the last. They believe that there are no other or better beliefs than theirs. It is similar to the man who went to the same place every year for his holiday and did not understand that their was a different holiday just as good.

Let us not make the same mistake with regard to our worship and let us explore different types, as we do our holidays, until we find something that is satisfactory. Above all, let us use our intelligence because we have been given a free will to think for ourselves so let us do so, by asking questions and investigating for ourselves.

Alpha

We call this Alpha because this was the beginning and it is written in answer to the number of questions we have been asked about how we became involved in spiritualism. Hello to you, my name is George Knight and we would like to take you back to the time before we knew anything of spiritualism. We go right back to Christmas 1936.

At that time, my father who had suffered ill health for many years, had a nasty turn which took him into some sort of coma. Whilst in this state, an angelic smile covered his face and he said the words of a famous old hymn, 'When the roll is called up yonder, I'll be there.' My father recovered from this attack but three months later in the month of March he passed away. After this my mother became interested in spiritualism but personally I thought it was a load of rubbish.

The Second World War started and we had to join the Forces, but, towards the end of the war, we were stationed in Plymouth where we met three sisters who were also interested in spiritualism and, although we spoke about the subject, I never took up their invitation to go to church. The spirit friends must have had their eyes on me even then.

When I came home on leave my mother said that she was going to a circle at someone's house and if I wanted I could go and, although at first I declined, I eventually went.

I was placed so that I was sitting right opposite the medium and there followed a period of meditation and the medium then went into what I now know was a trance condition. As I watched, the medium's face changed and a beautiful smile came over it and then came the words, 'When the roll is called up yonder, I'll be there.' I just went rigid. People have said that my mother had probably told him what my father had said but even if we accept this, how did he produce the smile that came over his face?

After nine years this was a terrific shock because we could not fathom how this man repeated something that had happened so long ago. We came to the conclusion that there must be something in it after all. No wonder they say that God moves in a mysterious way.

We were fortunate to be accepted into a circle and since then have been involved in many circles and groups with the hope that we have been able to give as much help as we have received. In those early days we were attached to one particular church but after a number of years we left and moved to fresh fields. This was part of our progression because by leaving we gathered more knowledge, whereas if we had stayed we would have been in a rut.

Some time later, we became involved with another church but, again, after a period of time we moved on. These experiences were lessons not only for us but also for the churches because we like to think that both sides learned something from our associations.

For many years we have not been associated with any one particular church but visit many to give an address about spirituality and spiritual gifts. Of course, through clairvoyance we are allowed to demonstrate these gifts and we say allowed because without the guides and helpers we would not be able to do these things.

To develop these gifts, we all have to sit and learn in a very sincere way, being ready to make sacrifices, not only financially. In fact, we are still studying and learning because remember that no one on this earth will ever finish reading the book of life. We are always sorry to hear of people who have read a couple of chapters and think that is sufficient. Through this studying we have learned how to meditate quietly, to endeavour to shut out all noises: we hate all noise. We have done this meditation for many years now on a daily basis sitting quietly every morning and we find we can face anything that the day may bring forth. Through this meditation, we are now able to keep our ears, our eyes and, most important, our mouths shut when it is necessary. If we can all try to achieve this then our minds are clear and open to receive inspiration from the spirit friends. Let us remember that most of the ideas and brainwaves we get start in the spirit world.

Over the years since becoming involved in spiritualism we seem to have taken a deeper interest in nature and feel that by studying plants, flowers, trees, birds and animals we have learned spiritual lessons. By observing how the animals leave their young to fend for themselves we realise that each one of us must not lean on others but know that we are responsible for our own thoughts and actions. When we all face this truth we than know that our spiritual progress is on our own hands.

We also know there is a seedtime and a harvest and in between these the soil goes through many changes such as the effects of snow, frost, rain and shine. This again is similar to our lives because we experience all kinds of weather as our progression is made.

Personally I have noticed that when the material side is suffering the frost and snows then the spiritual side begins to experience the sun and gentle rain. The meaning of this is that when our material is low then the spiritual starts to rise.

As we become willing to let the seasons pass then we find we are developing patience and in so doing are willing to let events take their course rather than forcing things. It also brings a peace and happiness, a calmness whereby we have trust in our spirit friends. My wife says that if the roof fell in I would not worry, and the reason I mention this is that I wish others could experience this peace and calmness.

Spiritualism has given me a philosophy that says all wealth should be shared and by this I mean our good fortune, love, compassion, knowledge and gifts. It is no good being able to paint masterpieces if they are going to be kept in a cellar where no one can see them, it is no good being a fine musician if no one is never going to hear us play. We all have spiritual gifts so let others benefit from our use of them.

Personal responsibility we have to take on board for our journey through life and this means that whatever we do is our decision and we cannot blame others for any consequences arising from our thoughts and actions. So let us think positively, work honestly and always show love and compassion. Do not cheat others because, by so doing, we are only cheating ourselves as we will discover when we leave this earth. Let us remember that it is no good asking God to forgive us if we are not willing to forgive others.

If we practise these things we shall be rich in the things that matter – happiness, contentment and peace of mind. That is what my journey into spiritualism has taught me.